# The Transformation

# The | Transformation Factor

## TOWARDS AN ECOLOGICAL CONSCIOUSNESS

### ALLERD STIKKER

## ELEMENT

Rockport, Massachusetts ● Shaftesbury, Dorset
Brisbane, Queensland

© 1992 Allerd Stikker

Published in the U.S.A. in 1992 by
Element, Inc.
42 Broadway, Rockport, MA 01966

Published in Great Britain in 1992 by
Element Books Limited
Longmead, Shaftesbury, Dorset

Published in Australia in 1992 by
Element Books Ltd for
Jacaranda Wiley Ltd
33 Park Road, Milton, Brisbane, 4064

Cover design by Barbara McGavin
Text design by Roger Lightfoot
Typeset by BP Integraphics
Printed in the United States of America by
Edwards Bros

Library of Congress Cataloging-in-Publication Data

Stikker, Allerd, 1928–
   [Tao, Teilhard en westers denken. English]
   The transformation factor: towards an ecological
   consciousness
Allerd Stikker.
   Translation of: Tao, Teilhard en westers denken.
   Includes bibliographical references.
1. Teilhard de Chardin, Pierre.   2. Philosophy,
Taoist.   3. Human ecology–Religious aspects.
4. Human ecology–Philosophy.   5. Cosmology.
I. Title.
B2430  T374S7913  1992
194–dc20     91–28371

British Library Cataloguing in Publication Data

A catalogue record for this book is
available from the British Library

ISBN 1-85230-271-2

# Contents

*Foreword by Joseph Needham*   ix

*Preface*   1

*Introduction*   5

PART ONE

Taoism, Teilhard de Chardin and Western
Thought: A Comparison

Chapter 1    Distinction and Unity   10

Chapter 2    Change   40

Chapter 3    Human Values   61

Chapter 4    Conclusions from the Comparison   75

PART TWO

Applying the Views of the Taoists and
Teilhard de Chardin in Today's World

Chapter 5    Emerging Worldview   80

Chapter 6    Present Trends in the World   89

Chapter 7    Options for Action   118

*Conclusion*   122

*Notes*   129

*Select Bibliography*   135

If the dynamics of the universe from the beginning shaped the course of the heavens, lighted the sun, and formed the earth – if this same dynamism brought forth the continents and seas and atmosphere, if it awakened life in the primordial cell and then brought into being the unnumbered variety of living beings and finally brought man into being and guided him safely through the turbulent centuries – there is reason to believe that this same guiding process is precisely what has awakened in man his present understanding of himself and his relation to this stupendous process. Sensitized to this guidance we can have confidence in the future that awaits the human venture.

THOMAS BERRY
From *The New Story*, Teilhard Studies N° 1, 1978.

# Foreword

It is a privilege to have been asked to contribute a foreword to Allerd Stikker's fascinating monograph, though truly it needs none.

Brought up in the bosom of the Western capitalist world, first as a chemical engineer, then as a business man, Stikker became more and more disenchanted with the prevailing philosophical assumptions of the West, seeing that many of them would inevitably lead to disaster for humankind. By contrast, two systems particularly impressed him, two systems at opposite ends, as it were, of history: that of the Taoist philosophers in ancient China, and that of Pierre Teilhard de Chardin in our own time. Stikker's book luminously explains the similarities and the differences between these two.

The extraordinary thing is that although Teilhard spent many years in China, he had no direct connection (so far as we know) with modern Chinese scholars who could have explained Taoism to him. Teilhard must have been isolated in the expatriate community of pre-World War II days.

The Taoists were writing long before modern science came into existence, and long before it had arrived at a perception of the evolutionary process, cosmic and inorganic preceding biological evolution, and biological evolution preceding social evolution in a succession of palpably increasing complexity and organization.

Teilhard, on the other hand, began as a paleontologist and turned into one of the greatest prophets of our times, contending that Christians—and indeed the adherents of all the great religions—must take evolution seriously. Teilhard never gave up his Christianity, and always affirmed the characteristic Christian belief in a divine creator; but he put religion in the cadre of the evolutionary process, and saw the *Regnum Dei* as its

assured outcome. In the course of this, he developed a mysticism of matter, and urged a fundamentally world-affirming
attitude, very different from that of so many of the fathers and
saints of the early Church. They could not have been expected to
understand an evolutionary process—but neither could the
Taoists, yet they worked out by insight and vision a world
scheme that was entirely compatible with evolutionary
thinking.

For example, they affirmed the integrality of humanity with
nature. The Tao was the Order of Nature; you could call it the
immanent deity. The Taoists declined to make any distinction
between matter and spirit; heaven, earth and man (*thien, ti jen*)
were inter-dependent. They praised the virtues of water (which
wears away the hardest things) and the feminine (which knows
how to observe passively, yet does not force things into obedi-
ence). The old Chinese dualism was quite different from that of
Persia, for the *summum bonum* consisted in the most perfect
balance between the yin and the yang, never identifying the
good with one and evil with the other.

The Scientific Revolution happened in Europe in the seventeenth century, and in Europe only. It led before long to
mechanistic thinking and a reductionism to which none of the
ethnically oriented medieval sciences had given rise. This was
an inevitable result of the mathematization of hypotheses about
nature combined with relentless experimentation. Thus, there
arose a division, humanity separated from nature, yet by the
very onward march of science itself, evolution theory put
humankind back into its place as part of nature. Now its integration with nature has gone even further, as one can see by the
essential role of the observer in quantum mechanics.

The Taoists of old never had any doubts that human beings
were part of nature, and the Tao ran through all. As Stikker says:
''Teilhard restored again, after two thousand years of dialectical
and conflicting Western thinking, the unity and interdependence that the Chinese philosophers sensed by intuition and
spontaneity.'' He goes on to write that the visions of the old
Taoists and of Teilhard are both of great interest for the development and maturation of modern thought. Combined, they
present an even stronger case, either by mutual reinforcement
when they converge, or by the appearance of complementary
values when they diverge.

In the last part of his book, Allerd Stikker applies some of these insights to current trends in world affairs, often quantitatively depicted, some of which will lead humankind down "the primrose path to the everlasting bonfire" if not checked—and soon. I do not necessarily agree with Stikker in all his judgments on the course of the history of science in China, on current political affairs or on the Chinese concepts of time. However, that does not alter my belief that he has done an excellent service to world thought in comparing the ideas of the old Taoists, Lao Tzu and Chuang Tzu, with those of Teilhard de Chardin. I wish his book every success.

Joseph Needham FRS, FBA

# Preface

It may be useful for the reader of this book to know how I came to write on this subject and what I expect to achieve with it.

I grew up in a family with wise, hard working and pragmatic parents. We had no formal connection with any religious institution and, although I lived in a society where Christianity was the cultural history, I never received any instruction in Christian belief.

My formal education began with secondary school at the Barlaeus Gymnasium in Amsterdam, during World War II. After the war, I studied chemical engineering at The Delft Institute of Technology in Holland. I chose this training because I was interested in industrial activity. During my secondary education I also had become fascinated with chemistry and with the discovery that matter could be transformed from one type, shape and color into another type, shape and color, just by mixing in the right proportions at the right temperature and pressure and with the right catalyst. It aroused in me the awareness that there was a fundamental dynamic aspect in our physical surroundings.

During my studies at Delft, I began to feel uncomfortable with the basic principles of physics and mathematics necessary to integrate chemistry into an engineering science. Although I could follow and apply intellectually the methods and exercises to formulate mathematical and mechanical relationships, I became mentally opposed to the notion that everything can be calculated, measured, predicted and controlled. I could not believe that there were no other influences governing the course of events in this world.

In 1949 I came across a book by Lecomte du Noüy called, *Human Destiny*; I still have the copy I read at that time. It completely revolutionized my thinking. My eyes were opened to the fact that the universe, the earth and humankind are involved in a dynamic process of continuous transformation, not only materially and biologically, but also spiritually.

I learned that this process follows a pattern, that there is a basic universality in the building blocks throughout all of nature, that there is a direction and that there were and are, in the process, leaps of discontinuity. I became aware of a dynamic unfolding of the total universe and of the place of our planet and humanity in this universal process. This new dimension of consciousness and its broad scope could accommodate all of the various religions, philosophies and scientific explanations that confront us today. This new dimension also accommodates mysticism as the process includes both rational and irrational elements. There is unity in diversity at a higher level. This new unity evokes the feeling of unknown forces in a universal interdependence of everything that happens. How can this process be translated into a coherent vision for humanity today?

The fact that I was never confronted with a specific philosophy of life or a specific religious doctrine in my youth enabled me to be open and unbiased to new thinking. On the other hand, I think that my personal development and that of my contemporaries would have benefitted greatly from more education in the history of religious and scientific thinking. Such education needs to emphasize contemporary cultural and political developments, with awareness of the philosophical implications throughout specific periods in time.

In 1963, I read for the first time *The Phenomenon of Man*, the English translation of *Le Phénomène Humain*, by Pierre Teilhard de Chardin. I was struck by the inspiring message that humanity and our planet are engaged in a huge and dynamic process of evolution, with a direction and a purpose. The brilliant synthesis by the Jesuit priest Teilhard of religion, philosophy and science within a historical and futuristic perspective was, for me, a revelation.

During my international business travels, I came across a third 'revelation': the philosophical works of the early Taoists in China. I was mentally and emotionally impressed by the remarkable insight and foresight they developed about the human being, the earth and the universe. There were also intriguing relationships between Taoists' philosophy and Teilhard de Chardin's vision, although from a different perspective in time and knowledge. It is remarkable that Teilhard, who spent twenty-three years in China as a paleontologist, did not tap directly this vast reservoir of ancient wisdom and originality.

I became convinced that a combination of the spontaneous and intuitive visions of the Taoist philosophers and the constructive, unifying and evolutionary visions of Teilhard could give today's world citizen a wealth of new and refreshing ideas on the moral, philosophical and religious approach of the world today. It had become clear to me that a fundamental philosophy is lacking in the approach by individuals to living, by politicians to governing, by managers to leading, by teachers to educating and by religions to guiding the life of citizens on this earth.

Many people, old and young, have unsatisfactory feelings about their visions of life. However, they have (and take) no time to think about that vision, even though they find the way the subject is presented by the church or by science or philosophy complicated, confusing and inadequate. Deep in their hearts, however, they yearn for inspiring guidance as they search for fulfillment during this passage on earth.

I decided to make a 'progress report' (or should it be process report?) on impressions about where we stand today in the Western world, primarily to satisfy my personal need for guidance and possibly to provide some directions to readers of this study. I am convinced that humanity is heading for a new major leap in the evolutionary process. A thorough understanding of what the Taoists, Teilhard de Chardin and the latest visions in physics and ecology are telling us will help us to become aware of this process. The scientific, political, industrial, economic, religious and educational institutions of human society are hardly aware of a new transformation, yet they will be involved in the next leap, so they had better be prepared.

During the preparation for this book, I received, on the subjects of Taoism and Teilhard, very valuable advice and encouragement from Soeur Marie Ina Bergeron, Ph.D., in Paris, Father Thomas Berry, Ph.D. and Prof. Ewert H. Cousins, Ph.D., in New York, Dr. Frits Bottcher in Holland, Dr. Ursula King in Leeds, Dr. Joseph Needham in Cambridge and Father Yves Raguin, S.J., in Taipei.

I would like to thank my family who contributed so much to my development and who endure the consequences of my restless search along the road of discovery. This holds also for my closest and true friends.

# Introduction

With this book, I would like to reach people who are not necessarily specialists in the subjects of religion, philosophy or science. It contains an attempt to give the reader food for thought on the simple question most human beings put to themselves from time to time: Who am I and what am I doing here?

The old Chinese Taoist philosophers had some very interesting responses to this question, based on intuitive, spontaneous and original thinking. The Western world lost much of the intuition, spontaneity, and originality concerning this question because Christian and scientific attitudes increasingly alienated the human being from nature. Pierre Teilhard de Chardin was the first Western thinker to restore an effective unity in the diverging forces that are influencing Western humanity. He reconciled the diversity of forces within the unity and dynamics of the evolutionary process.

In this study, an attempt is made to detect common denominators in Chinese and Teilhardian thinking, portrayed against the background of Western thinking as it developed over the last two thousand years. This will be done on the basis of major issues, selected by the author, confronting humanity. Preliminary conclusions result from this approach, submitting a coherent but open-ended view with respect to earth, the human being and the universe today. The viewpoint I present can be helpful for individual contemplation and development as well as for collective actions and strategies.

There is an abrupt transition from the contemplative nature of the first part of the study to the hard facts of our world of today as presented in the second part. The object of the study is to show that there is a clear relationship between our philosophical, cultural, scientific and religious history and the present state of the world. The present state of the world is illustrated by factual selections from global reports on the social, economic, industrial and political developments of the 1980s and projections for the year 2000. The mentality and format of decision-making by the major institutions today are inadequate to cope with emerging problems of imbalance created by innovative technological and organizational developments in the West. These have led to improved material standards of living, but also to the growing alienation of humanity from nature. This course could lead to the destruction of our planet. My study attempts to show how the Western world arrived on this course, how our present position relates to the past and how the alienation can be reversed by applying Taoist and Teilhardian visions to our Western culture.

The explorations of the past and the present then will be linked to ideas and visions that have been developed recently in the United States and Europe. The 'new thinking' is based on the sophisticated awareness of the potentiality of an imminent major transformation in the evolutionary process of our planet within fifty years, and upon the need to recognize the necessary conditions for such a transformation: restoring individual harmony and the dynamic balance of humanity's relationship with nature on a local and global scale.

The object of the study is to show that there is a coherence between Taoist, Teilhardian and new Western thinking, and that humanity is capable of progressing on a clear path towards a new transformation. Individual involvement and collective responsibilities greatly influence the direction and the quality of the path and the transformation. It is therefore necessary for as many people as possible to have access to and awareness of the knowledge we have developed collectively through the ages concerning our role on earth and in the universe.

Western society has been highly creative and innovative culturally, scientifically and technologically. It must not regress, but the degree of saturation of its present state of development with increasingly undesirable side effects, and thus the need for change, provides an opening for incorporating essential Taoist and Teilhardian thinking in the creation of a new story, a new order, built on the achievements of the past and oriented toward a higher level of coordination and harmony.

The material used for the analysis of Taoist and Teilhardian thinking is predominantly of a specialized kind. Not only are the contents sometimes complicated, but the language requires much re-reading and the words used are often rare in common language. I have no knowledge of Chinese characters and speech, and have only read English and French translations of the Chinese texts. However, it is still possible to grasp the main ideas of the specialized literature without being or becoming an expert.

The reader of this book does not need any knowledge of Taoist philosophy or Teilhard de Chardin's work. The simplified approach of this study will undoubtedly raise some eyebrows because it condenses whole chapters in history that played a vital role in reaching present levels of knowledge and understanding. The aim is to make the main thoughts and their interconnections available to the layperson; it is regrettable and unnecessary that so much of the experience that has been acquired and written in humanity's history remains inaccessible to the majority because of language difficulties. I have tried to avoid the use of language often found in literature of this kind; in many cases the issues can be treated in a common language, without having to resort to technical or scholarly words that are only understood by a small circle. Where developments in science and specifically physics are introduced in the text, the use of some technical terms is unavoidable. This should not discourage the nontechnical reader.

The Chinese philosophy has been extracted from works of Chinese philosophers from the period 500 B.C. and A.D. 1200 such as Kung Fu Tzu (circa 500 B.C.), Lao Tzu (circa 400 B.C.), Chuang Tzu (circa 350 B.C.), Huai Nan Tzu (circa 150 B.C.), Lieh Tzu (circa 50 B.C.), Wang Pi (circa A.D. 250) and Chu Hsi (circa A.D. 1150).

The Teilhardian vision is mostly derived from his basic works, such as *Phenomenon of Man* and *The Divine Milieu*, published after his death in 1955, and partly from works by various authors on Teilhard's thought, and later publications of Teilhard's essays and letters.

The information on the current state of the world has been gathered from reports of the early 1980s by the World Bank, the Brandt Commission, OECD, United Nations and United States government agencies, and the World Watch Institute.

New ideas and visions of today have been found in publications by Marilyn Ferguson, Hazel Henderson, Barbara Marx Hubbard, Jean Houston, Thomas Berry, Fritjof Capra, Willis H. Harman, Robert Muller, Peter Russell and others.

In addition to these new ideas and visions, humanitarian consequences of important issues in new physics and related theories of very recent date are touched upon and are derived from the works of David Bohm, Ilya Prigogine and Rupert Sheldrake.

Information and opinions on decision-making in major institutions are based partly on personal experience and observation and partly on publications by corporations and consultants.

From the information and analysis presented, I have attempted to draw conclusions leading to a new view on the world and its future, and to offer options for reaching this future.

The study is relatively short and concise, I leave it to the reader to separately consult more extensive literature which is abundantly available in all the fields covered.

# Part One

Taoism, Teilhard de Chardin and Western Thought: A Comparison

# Distinction and Unity

"There was a thing, a 'gathering' chaos,
Which existed prior to heaven and earth.
Silent! Empty!
Existing by itself, unchanging,
Pervading everywhere, inexhaustible,
It might be called the mother of the world.
Its name is unknown,
I simply call it Tao.
If I were to exert myself to define it,
I might call it great.
Great means extending to the limitless.
Extending to the limitless means reaching the extreme distance.
Thus, Tao is great.
Heaven is great, earth is great, and man is great, too.
In the universe we have four greatnesses, and man is but one.
Man is in accordance with earth.
Earth is in accordance with heaven.
Heaven is in accordance with Tao.
Tao is in accordance with that which is."[1]

Thinking in terms of wholeness or of parts has dominated and influenced all human cultures. The importance of this issue and the way it was approached by the Taoists and Pierre Teilhard de Chardin is illustrated in the following observations. In the first section, the general background on distinctional and unified thinking is described. In later sections, the translation of this thinking into specific applications in the human search for truth is discussed. The last section deals with the origin and the return to the concept of oneness.

### Earth, Human Being and Universe

One of the most troubling aspects of the so-called Western developed civilizations in today's world is the distinction between earth, humanity and the universe. To be sure, with the advance of science, we have penetrated deeper into the structure of matter, organisms and the universe than ever before. We have discovered, in the last decennium, as many as two hundred subatomic particles, a far stretch from original concepts of the atom (a word derived from the Greek for indivisible). We have discovered the chemical composition of the most complicated components of living organisms as well as the chemical and physical processes that keep these organisms alive. We have been able to link some of these processes with the functioning of our own minds. We have discovered that the universe contains at least two billion galaxies such as the Milky Way, of which our sun is only a tiny star in the midst of hundreds of billions of other stars.

On the other hand, by the very methods used in all these discoveries, namely the analytical reduction of the objects of study into separate parts, we have developed a sense of radical distinctions which leads us to think of earth, humanity and universe as separate categories.

Paradoxically, Christianity, which has opposed science and separated the secular and divine worlds, helped create fertile soil for science to develop the mentality of compartmental thinking.

Christian belief differentiates body and soul, the world and God, matter and spirit. This pattern of differentiation originates from a period of thought transformation that took place between 800 and 200 B.C., when a new thinking emerged almost simultaneously in several parts of the world. The philosophies of Plato and Aristotle in Greece, the prophecies of Elijah, Isaiah and Jeremiah in Palestine, the revelations of Buddha and the Upanishads in India, the wisdom of Confucius and Lao Tzu in China, and the dualism of Zoroaster in Persia represent these new patterns of thought. All of the new thinking shared an increasing consciousness of individual critical reflection and started to replace, to a certain extent, the mythology of the previous tribal periods.

Except in Taoism, these developments led to envisioning two radically distinct worlds, the physical and the metaphysical, with varying degrees of interrelatedness. Karl Jaspers called this remarkable coincidental "leap" in human thinking the "axial period."[2]

Plato and Aristotle envisioned a basic harmony of the universe. Aristotle considered the universe as one total organism.

Both were interested in understanding not only the "what" and the "how", but also the "why." The emphasis, however, in both philosophies is on the mind, the idea, the "logos" as the ultimate reality. Aristotle, more than and after Plato, was also interested in the physical world and nature. Aristotle, however, remained a strong advocate of the primacy of the mind, the spirit. He also made a distinction between the subject and the object. This notion had great influence on later scientific, philosophical and religious developments in the West.

A similar distinction between the spiritual real world and the illusionary material world (*Maya*) in Buddhism and Hinduism influenced the religious developments of the East. The original, philosophical vision in Taoism was different and unique in that it did not lead to these distinctions. This is a reason that Buddhism as such, although very influential, was never accepted in China. When Buddhism came to China in the first part of the last millennium, it was adapted to the world-affirmative and harmony model of Taoism.

In the West, Platonic and Aristotelean thinking, and later neo-Platonic thinking, led to an ambiguous combination of radical distinctions and mysticism. These were important elements in the later development of Western scientific Christian thinking. St. Thomas Aquinas formulated the Christian thinking in his *Summa contra Gentiles*, written in the thirteenth century in the same period as his *Summa Theologica*; both are still the fundamental works of Catholic thinking today. These works are based primarily on concepts and judgments, logic and reason, systematic and abstract thought as developed by Greek philosophy. There is little place for intuition and myth.

In the same period, Bonaventure, the influential Franciscan thinker, wrote a theological synthesis strongly influenced by Francis of Assisi's love of nature.[3] He maintained a synthesis between theology, mysticism and the world, avoiding the notion of radical distinctions. His integral theological vision has been interpreted as embodying the principle of the *coincidentia oppositorium* or coincidence of opposites related through complementarity, in a way that is similar to the complementarity of Taoism. However, his works were obscured, being overshadowed by the sheer power and popularity of Thomism.

From the sixteenth century on, attention in the West became increasingly focused on the material world. This originated from the concept of the mundane world as being separate from God, with the supposition that the world was governed from outside through divinely guaranteed and fixed patterns. In order to understand the purpose and the ways of God, Western thinking attempted to know these patterns and invented "laws." This was done primarily through analyzing, reducing and measuring the material and natural world. In the seventeenth century, much to the dismay of the Church, the emphasis changed increasingly from divine patterns to the material laws.

The "mechanistic" worldview began to dominate in the Western world. The term "mechanistic" is meant to describe the attitude that everything in the universe can be reduced to matter and movement, excluding any other influence. The early exponents of this movement, such as Isaac Newton and Francis Bacon, were deeply religious in their thinking and life-styles, and they were aware of the risks involved in this view. However, discovery was in the atmosphere of the age. Christian religion, which emphasized the concrete history of the arrival of Jesus Christ and the doctrines of the Fall and the Redemption and their implication of developmental human time, provoked the urge to investigate direction and purpose in the divine process. Until the seventeenth century, the Church had cooperated with scientific thought in the context of two separate worlds: the physical one and the metaphysical. The turn to materialistic and mechanistic dominance in science now led to alienation between science and religion. This further reinforced the tendency to think in terms of radical distinctions.

At this point, it is useful to leave the Western scene and investigate how Taoist thinking concerning the relationship between earth, human beings and universe developed. In the earliest Taoist writings, one is confronted with the fundamental viewpoint that radical distinctions between the physical and the metaphysical are created by the subjective observations of human beings. This early viewpoint is based on the notion that before anything existed at all there was the "indistinct": nothing is distinguished, not even nothingness. Although, by definition, this cannot be given a name, the idea of the "Tao" is supposed to indicate this notion. The Tao, sometimes called the Way, is the source of all being, all life, including human beings. The Tao is the basic, undivided unity in which all the contradictions and distinctions of existence ultimately are resolved.

The *Tao Te Ching,*[4] a scripture attributed to Lao Tzu, describes

Taoist philosophy in eighty-one short chapters. Here it becomes clear that the Chinese character for Tao has many different meanings, as it is the principle of everything, in everything and the origin of everything. Yet it is still undefinable and impersonal. In Taoist thinking, the Tao leads to One, One leads to Two (principles of yin and yang), Two leads to Three and the Ten Thousand Things, being all external manifestations in our world.

But the basic origin is unity, to which everything will return. The manifestations in our world are all dualistic, originating from the Two. The Two and all dualistic manifestations are not separated conflicting opposites, but complementary, interchanging and dynamic counterparts in a whole. They exist by the grace of their mutual existence: one pole would not exist if the other pole did not exist. So, the Taoist viewpoint is that radical distinctions do not exist.

Symbolically, one could picture the two visions of duality as follows:

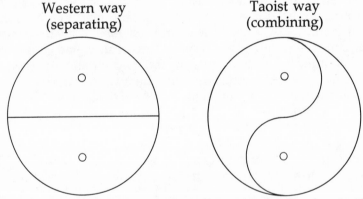

Western way
(separating)

Taoist way
(combining)

The latter is the historical symbol of Taoism. In the observations of the Taoist philosophers, earth, humanity and the universe are all part of the totality of a dynamic, coherent and interacting system. In that relationship there exists no hierarchy in the Christian sense. This means, for instance, that the human being, although especially gifted, is part of nature and not above nature. Life on earth is connected with the universal process, and throughout earthly existence living beings continually interact with the universe. The human being is, therefore, an integral part of the total system. In Taoism the human being lives in the universe through a positive experience of earthly existence. Taoist philosophy is world affirming, not world negating.

Within this line of thinking there is no law or fixed pattern imposed from outside the world. This is an important reason why in China, science did not develop as it did in the West. China was much earlier and much more advanced than the West in making use of technologies in practical applications of available material and natural processes. These technologies, such as acupuncture, were based on nature, not science. Taoist philosophy regarded natural processes and applications as part of, and implicit in, an internal order within the universe. The Taoists did not analyze natural processes, but accepted them as they manifested themselves.

Therefore, the radical distinction of the West and the shifting of the emphasis from the spiritual to the material world could not occur in China. The soil for such a development was not fertile, because human society in China was based on the unifying, humanistic doctrine of Confucius.

Today, in mainland China and in Taiwan especially, material emphasis is increasing strongly as science and science-based technologies are imported from the West. For the time being—and certainly among members of the younger generations—the old Chinese philosophies are generally disregarded. How this development will balance out within the context of a three-thousand-year-old culture remains to be seen. There are signs that the core of the culture is more resilient than outsiders realize, regardless of the fact that the present government of the People's Republic of China is focusing its policies exclusively on agriculture, industry, science and defense, the "four modernizations,"[5] with no place for the "humanities."

The divisive developments in the West were recognized by Pierre Teilhard de Chardin in the early 1920s as he developed his vision of the earth, humanity and the universe, culminating in *The Divine Milieu* and the *Phenomenon of Man*. Those works were written in China in 1928 and 1940, but were only published after Teilhard's death in 1955. His Order, the Jesuits, had opposed publication because his visions were considered in conflict with the teachings of the Catholic Church. It must be emphasized, however, that Teilhard himself considered his vision an enrichment and confirmation of his deep Christian belief.

An important dimension of Teilhard's vision was that he interpreted the story of Genesis to include an evolving dynamic universe—"cosmogenesis"—whereas biblical Genesis assumes a fixed universe. The foundation of his concept is that the whole of the cosmos is in a dynamic state of creative change, with mutual interdependence and interactions between the composing elements, without discontinuity. It is clear that such an approach does not allow for the separateness described in the beginning of this chapter.

The dynamic link between earth, humanity and the universe is presented most clearly in Teilhard's *The Divine Milieu*.[6] In this essay, he emphasizes that the human being is not isolated from and on earth but is part of the earth. As the earth is part of the universe, the human being is part of the universe through the earth. According to Teilhard's concept of cosmogenesis, the universe is unfolding continually into new and creative forms— with an intentionality. This is a very important model because it makes human existence on earth meaningful in the universal process, rather than a sinful journey in a material world that must be endured until redemption out of the world.

Teilhard's model emphasizes a creative rather than a redemptive attitude. It is world affirming, not world negating. Teilhard wholeheartedly preaches the active involvement of the individual in earthly activities. Through work on earth, the human can mature, become aware of the realities of nature and contribute to the development of individual and collective consciousness. In this way, two purposes are served: personal development on the microscale and the completion of the world on a macroscale, as part of cosmogenesis.

Teilhard observes the individual experiences of development and attachment (to earthly life), and retirement and detachment (towards the divine) as two perfectly compatible aspects in the system of Christian life. These two aspects of the human existence—involvement in the practical (micro) world and devotion to the universal (macro) whole (ultimate divine)—are intimately interconnected. Human beings can live in harmony and not in conflict with the two aspects. Teilhard sees the emphasis shift during the lifetime of the individual from attachment to detachment as the preparation for joining a new dimension after death. With regard to the visions on earth, human being and universe, Teilhard restored again, after two thousand years of dialectic and conflicting Western thinking, the unity and the interdependence that the Chinese philosophers sensed by intuition and spontaneity.

We find here a parallel in the universal or cosmological

approach of Taoism and Teilhard in a dynamic, harmonious, unified, and world affirming model. Teilhard apparently was not aware of this parallel. He did not spend much time on Chinese thought, because he felt that Eastern thinking was passive, world-negating and ignored evolution.

Teilhard's opinion was, on the other hand, that Eastern and Western thought should flow towards a richer world view through diversity in union.[7]

His reserved views on Eastern thinking become clear upon reading some of the rare texts that exist on this subject. Teilhard wrote a summary of this vision in 1947 and 1948 in Paris.[8] Other writers, including Ursula King, Claude Riviere and Dominique Wang, have recorded or analyzed his opinion on Eastern, including Taoist, thinking.

His attitude also should be seen against the background of his professional work in China. In his capacity as paleontologist, he predominantly met with modern Chinese scientists, European and American colleagues and, especially during the war, the diplomatic corps.

## Energy, Spirit and Matter

The concept of separateness or radical distinction, which has been mentioned earlier and which originated in what Karl Jaspers called the axial period (800–200 B.C.), has dominated Christian thinking on matter, spirit and energy. The general opinion was that our material world was imperfect and of secondary importance. The spiritual world, the mind's world was the true reality. What we were learning, seeing and touching in the material world was a distortion of the ultimate reality. The relationships between body and soul, matter and spirit, manifestations and mind, earth and heaven, human beings and God were debated and analyzed with confusing results.

We humans experience our personal egos in daily life, but we also sense that there is something else, undefinable but present, instinctively and intuitively there, not describable as our conscious world seems to be. We know that mathematical and geometrical formulations cannot, ultimately, explain all situations and forms. The story of Achilles who cannot overtake the turtle is a good illustration of the gap. The difference in distance between the two becomes smaller and smaller, but mathematically a small difference remains infinite. We know that Achilles will overtake the turtle, but we cannot mathematically describe the moment he "jumps" over the infinitely small, just as we cannot describe or understand the infinitely large. Both exist, but we cannot understand them with mathematical, mechanical intellect, which has developed models that do not describe the ultimate reality. What seems easier than to solve the deadlock by "inventing" two worlds? If we follow strictly mental concepts and these concepts fail to respond to what we observe, we can attempt to solve the conundrum with additional mental concepts that compensate for the failure. In this way, we continue to move in a circuit outside of nature! The West has invented two worlds (the earthly and the divine), and thereby paved the way to a world negating religion, ritualistic traditions, a covenant between humankind and God, a strong hierarchal Church organization and dogmatic concepts for the faithful. These faithful were seen to be incapable of coping, intellectually and mentally, with the mystery of the physical and spiritual aspects of life. Conversely, the intellectual concepts diminished the creative potential of mythic, archetypal and magic processes. Although the imaginative insight, the intuitive wisdom and the mystical aspect of the original Christian belief remained present, the Greek philosophical influence and the Roman legal and organizational systems had become predominant in Christian religion.

As the concept of spirit, soul and mind, separate from matter, body and earth, became more and more difficult to define, other explanations to support these notions were sought. Because they were directly related to the mystery of life, and life is related to movement, and movement is related to energy, energy became an important element in the field of non-matter. A special moving force concept was developed by the vitalists and the animists, such as the *élan vital* of Bergson.[9] The notion of psychic energy being related to cosmic energy was implied in the thoughts of Teilhard de Chardin and Carl G. Jung. These mental exercises were intended to explain and interrelate the inner energy of organisms, the mystery of creation and the sustenance of living matter.

A breakthrough in divisive thinking came with the relativity theories of Albert Einstein in physics and the holistic approach of Carl Jung in psychology during the first half of the twentieth century. Einstein showed that energy and matter are mutually interchangeable and interdependent. He also postulated that experiments are influenced by the observer, both through the observer's relative position and the method of observation.

Jung assumed that the mental processes in human beings are related to a complex of interdependent factors of collective and individual unconsciousness and consciousness, and cannot be linked to separate causes alone.

With these new approaches, Western thinking was moving rapidly in the direction of looking at matter and energy, consciousness and unconsciousness, as a total dynamic system of interdependent factors. The most recent findings in so-called subatomic physics confirm the correctness of this approach. At the micro level it becomes clear that the location of the observer and the measuring method are so dominant that the observation is not purely objective. Observations are probabilities of groups, not individual identities. What is observed by science and psychology through "laws" is the result of statistical averages on the basis of the law of the great numbers. When the physicist is confronted with elementary particles and the psychologist with the human individual, statistical laws no longer apply. Jung emphasized this notion strongly.[10]

The new discoveries in physics and psychology leading to synthesis instead of analysis, to integration instead of reduction, to relations instead of identities, to dynamic instead of static views, to universal forces instead of only local ones, are opening possibilities for breaking through the rigid boundaries that have developed in Western religions and scientific thinking. The new ideas eventually will resolve the confusion in Western society on subjects concerning life and nature and the relationship to the ultimate reality.

The Taoist philosophers did not worry about a split between matter and energy. Their strong belief in the fundamental unity of the cosmos transcended such dualistic thought. Their view was not pantheism, for they believed that the cosmos itself is identical with the ultimate origin, that creation is solely within the cosmos. The Taoist concept of unity was different from the Greek sense of unity which saw a radical distinction between matter and spirit.

Taoist thought is based on the preexistence of the indistinct unity out of which emerges the material force, *Ch'i*. Ch'i is the basic energy existing before manifestations. It also represents the material force that leads to the manifestations of the Ten

Thousand Things resulting from complementary duality. Therefore, Ch'i also denotes matter. Ch'i exists before matter, and is the
origin of matter and physical energy. The Chinese ideogram for
Ch'i can be translated into both matter and energy, a symbol that
denotes the basic unity between the two. This notion does not
exist in Western language. The ideogram for Ch'i also expresses
the flow of energy in the human body, the human energy or spirit.
In the Taoist exercises for harmony and control of the body, called
*T'ai chi chuan*, the major objective is to channel the Ch'i harmoni-
ously through the centers of the body so as to create a balance
between spirit and matter. The energy flows smoothly throughout the body, rather than collecting unnaturally in certain
locations causing tensions in the head, the neck, the back,
etcetera.

From these examples, it is obvious how fundamental in
Chinese thinking is the function of Ch'i, as the original, cosmic,
all pervasive energy. The manifestation of matter-energy as it
arises from the Ch'i is determined by *li*, the universal principle
or pattern. This concept was developed by the later Taoists and
neo-Confucianists, and is discussed in chapter 2, in the section
on transformation.

Joseph Needham, the great authority on Chinese thought,
remarks that the neo-Confucianists applied this concept of
li to organizational levels in nature.[11] The higher the level of
organization, the more manifest become the moral values and
ethical behavior that are intrinsically present in the universe.
Needham's description seems related to Teilhard's vision on
evolution and his law of complexity/consciousness (which will
be discussed later).

Teilhard considered energy the original and ever-present
dynamic element of the universe, inherent in our planet and life
itself. This is similar to the Chinese notion of Ch'i. According to
Teilhard, primordial energy is psychic energy, which differentiates later partly into manifestations of physical energy and
matter. He concluded, to the horror of many physical scientists
of his generation, that all elements of the universe (including
inert material) contain non-material traces, even if infinitely
small. Spirit is immanently present in matter. In *Human Energy*,
he states ''There is neither spirit nor matter in the world; the
'stuff of the universe' is spirit-matter. No other substance but
this could produce the human molecule.''[12] This is very close to

the Taoist concept of Ch'i, which also denotes spirit-matter.

Teilhard's theory holds that the nonmaterial aspect becomes increasingly manifest the more complex the composition of matter is. This interaction between the material and the spiritual accounts for the appearance of life, of consciousness and self-consciousness in the more complex manifestations in the universe. In our world, this culminates in the human.

Teilhard called the psychic, internal energy the "radial" or "axial" force and the physical, external energy the "tangential" force. He considered the radial force the primary, consistent and evolutionary one, becoming apparent in the development of mind and consciousness. The tangential force, he believed, led to physical/chemical formations and complexities, which are material manifestations interacting with the psychic energy.

However, as he states in *The Phenomenon of Man*, "To avoid a fundamental dualism, at once impossible and anti-scientific, and at the same time to safeguard the natural complexity of the stuff of the universe, I accordingly propose that, essentially, all energy is physical in nature; but add that . . . this fundamental energy is divided in two distinct components: a *tangential energy* . . . and a *radial energy*.[13]

His major conviction and concern were that human energy, the zest for life, the urge to create, this self-organizing spirit, should be maintained, stimulated and fostered above everything else, if humans were to fulfill their role in the evolutionary process. This human energy is related to psychic energy. In the physical sciences in the last fifteen years, this energy has been assumed to be directly related to the energy of the original "fireball" at the birth of the universe.

There is a remarkable similarity between the Taoist view of energy and matter and Teilhard's ideas. Both consider these phenomena as being different forms of the same substance. Both also see the psychic and the physical energies as two complementary manifestations of the same basic substance. Teilhard, in his complexity-consciousness concept, introduces a pattern within which matter and energy interact, leading to different levels of orientation. Here we can see a similarity to the li principle.

### External and Internal Phenomena

The separatist attitude that is held in the Western world concerning the tangible and intangible, and the shift in emphasis to the tangible has had great influence on the life-style of Western society. The approach to daily life has become more externally and technically oriented. One obvious example of this is the West's fascination with machines and instruments, which led to the industrial revolution in the nineteenth century and the overwhelming influence industry maintains today.

An emphasis on quantity led to mechanization of and concentration of production into centralized groups. The economy of scale led to ever greater size; science and technology to a large extent were geared to promote this development. This emphasis on material and size led to a society that accorded the highest priority to these factors. Industrial concentration led to new power structures and to the alienation of the individual from the final product to which his contribution became more and more anonymous.

Karl Marx's protest against this development in the nineteenth century was a legitimate concern and remains so. However, the Western world never ran into the fundamental breakdown he predicted, nor did Marx's successors ever apply his basic idea of a democratic proletarian state. Over the long term, the capitalist system improved the standard of living of the average citizen steadily and consistently. In communist states, power was just transferred from one elite to another while the majority of citizens became more oppressed than ever. In the West, social protests were subordinated to the attraction of so-called welfare. It is in this atmosphere that Western society developed and that the elements of philosophy and religion gave way to politics and ideology.

Modern Western politics has moved toward short-lived governments with constantly changing emphases in economical and social, military and technological, local and global developments. Their objectives and functioning tend to be short-term and voter-oriented.

Ideologies such as communism, socialism and capitalism are becoming confusing for the average citizen who cannot comprehend fully their objectives and methods. Moreover, the language of ideology often dates back to periods in history that are long past and obsolete. Capitalism today is much more socially conscious than it was in the nineteenth century. Socialism, in Western and Eastern Europe, is becoming increasingly aware of the dangers of confusing equality of individual rights with equality of individual excellence. Communism is introducing the principles of market economy and private enterprise. While the politicians are still using language of the past and the national and international power struggles are still continuing, there seems to be an underlying trend of convergence and toward finding a balance between individual and collective rights and obligations.

Today we are living in a society whose orientation is strongly external. The ornaments and apparent wealth formerly reserved for royalty and nobility have become part of the daily life of the successful citizen and the ultimate goal of a great number of people. These developments are labeled as progress, but we need to evaluate the meaning of progress. Clearly the improvements in medical care, education and social security represent progress. On the other hand, individuals are growing increasingly uneasy. Instinctively we know that the increasing emphasis on external, material and military display is becoming out of balance with human nature, the nature of earth and the nature of the universe. Again, there is a gap between humanity, earth and universe.

Progress in recent decades is considered to be related to growth; increasingly, the result has been growth for the sake of growth. Growth is the major source for absorbing the ever-increasing cost elements of welfare and well-being: manpower, capital and, since the energy crisis in 1973, energy. To be sure, on the microscale there definitely have been developments where these increasing costs could be compensated by innovative and qualitative processes. Macro-economically, however, the quantitative growth process or mass economy as Paul Hawken calls it in his original and enlightening analysis of this phenomenon,[14] is the dominating factor.

Progress in the sense of quantitative growth is the paradigm of Western civilization. Like every paradigm in any discipline, it is defended with force and emotion, in this case by the industrial/political system, in spite of signs that it has reached its limits. Kuhn has identified this resisting force as a recurring phenomenon when outdated paradigms are under attack.[15] Especially in the field of science and philosophy, the established and respected representatives of accepted paradigms historically have resisted rigorously fundamental change or leaps up to the very last moment, until the process of change became irreversible.

Today the change will be from mass economy to informative

economy, from quantity to quality, from linear to nonlinear, from waste to endurance. Change also will be accomplished by eliminating overgrown intermediary institutions designed to do things that people increasingly can and will handle themselves. This will be stimulated by computer technology and increasing consciousness of ecological relationships. We will shift our emphasis from growing big to growing up. We will wake up from the American TV dream and discover the realities of a new world, maybe the world that was foreseen by the founders of the United States: "Novus ordo seclorum; annuit coeptis" (as it says today on the one dollar bill) meaning "The new order of the ages; (He) approves of this enterprise."

Taoist thinkers, such as Lao Tzu and Chuang Tzu, were driven by the conviction that the most important resources for harmonious living on this earth are within the human being and within nature. They claimed that a person who distances him or herself from external influences, seeks no recognition, shows no pride and follows his or her own pattern can be in balance internally, and through that balance can be in tune with the environment and the universe.

Confucius, on the other hand, emphasized the importance of the human organization, the moral structure and rules of behavior. In other words, he stressed an orientation toward formality and external performance.

The Taoists were of the opinion that one cannot regulate human society if one does not understand nature and how human beings relate to nature. The Confucianists, however, doubted the value of exploring the order of nature so long as the order of humanity was still far from perfect.

The Taoists believed that the most harmonious way to function on earth was to be as near as possible to the original unity: the Tao that is within you, from which you originated. Every step away from this leads to a less natural situation. Lao Tzu formulates in chapter 38 of *Tao Te Ching*[16] in the following sequence: "if you lose the Tao, you have the virtue; if you lose the virtue, you have humanity; if you lose humanity, you have righteousness; if you lose righteousness, you have rules of conduct." This is the sequence of a shift from internal to external, leading eventually to disorder: "Rules of conduct are due to lack of trustworthiness and are the beginning of disorder."

The Taoists recommended that the individual concentrate on

moving from the outer manifestations back to the origin, the inner self. In their view, the newly born human individual, through confrontation with the outer world, initially is developing and differentiating in the external direction, which results in dualities. By reversing the direction later, unity is regained.

Throughout his works, Teilhard emphasizes what he calls the interiority and the exteriority of all phenomena in the universe. All manifestations have internal and external aspects. With respect to the exteriority of things, he differentiates not only form, shape and size, but also complexity.

He illustrated this with a graph[17] (see Figure 1.1).

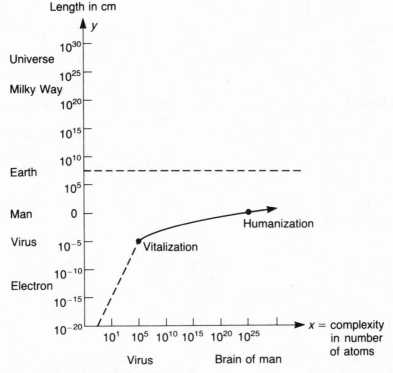

FIGURE 1.1   Approximation of relation between linear size and complexity (expressed in number of atoms in the complex). The asymptotic nature of the curve with relation to the size of the earth is meant to indicate that the human and humanity are, to our knowledge, the only and highest manifestation of complexity in the universe, on the planetary level.

With this schematic presentation, Teilhard wanted to express his viewpoint that while the external aspects of the phenomena are and can be quantified in size and configurations, from the very large to the very small, these are only quantitative, mechanistic descriptions of accumulations of material building blocks resulting from limited numbers of specific physical and chemical patterns. However, interior potentiality and nonmaterial patterns within these configurations become manifest when they reach certain complexity levels.

These are manifestations of basic psychic forces that are present in matter and in living creatures. The human being can be aware of this interior force because of the phenomenon of self-consciousness, which only manifests itself in the super-complex system of the human nervous system. Self-consciousness is meant to express the capability of being conscious of one's surroundings as well as of one's self.

Teilhard makes clear with his presentation of the law of complexity/consciousness, that the human species is a unique creation within the universe. We may be impressed with the infinitely small that we have discovered in subatomic physics; we may be overwhelmed by the incredible depth and vastness of the universe with its more than two billion galaxies; but we should not let ourselves be carried away by the sheer aspect of size and quantity. In complexity we find the ultimate subtlety of the universe, fragile, interdependent, highly volatile and evolutive. Here we can see the link with Prigogine's concept of the creative potential in complex systems that are far from equilibrium.[18]

Teilhard recognizes the uniqueness of the individual person, who, through self-consciousness, should be able to maintain harmony between quality and quantity, between the within and the without. He proposes that through the creative works of individuals and their combined efforts on this earth, the future of our planet is now being shaped. An essential element in his vision is the change, in the course of the human life, from earthy occupations and attachment, to divine orientations and detachment. Here we notice a clear parallel to the Taoist return to the origin, the inner self. It is clear from Teilhard's vision that continued emphasis on size and quantity, which are external appearances, will not lead to a harmonious and balanced future. The parallel between Teilhardian and Taoist thinking on harmony between quantity and quality, between attachment and detachment, strengthens the case for reconsideration of the present course of Western civilization.

## Human Being and Nature

As the modern world became more and more accepting of a view that separates the earth, humanity and the universe, matter and spirit, exteriority and interiority, this bifurcation alienated organic relationships between nature, life, humanity and spirit. Humanity is seen as distinct from and superior to nature, instead of being in and part of nature. This led to a cultural attitude where natural resources are to be used, transformed, controlled and directed. The mechanistic philosophy of science reinforced this attitude, and up into our present time the conquest of nature by humanity is hailed as a triumph.

Rationality ignores the book of nature. The origin of this attitude can be traced to the spirit of Plato; instead of the mystic primacy of the earth and the cosmos, his view was that we just have to understand the laws. The drive for knowledge led to objectification of nature and its dominance by the subject versus a subjective communion with nature.

The botanists and conservationists of the seventeenth century were driven by homocentric motivation. Everything was judged according to human usefulness.

In later industrial developments, technology bypassed the process of the biosphere. There was no awareness or concern for the impact of microscale developments, such as building local industrial complexes, on the macroscale environment of the planet. This could be done—and continued for quite some time—because of the relatively small effect of these intrusions upon nature. However, the exponential growth of industrial development led to an explosive growth of industrial complexes. The macroeffects are now becoming apparent and are of central importance. It now can be demonstrated quantitatively that the natural resources and the number of species of the earth are exponentially and irreversibly diminishing because of artificial elimination without compensation or renewal. Generally speaking, the conditions of life on earth are being destroyed. This process is fundamentally different from previous periods of evolution, natural selection and compensation, because it is taking place within one hundred years instead of billions of years.

Yet there is very little effective awareness of this development and solutions are inadequate, localized, corrective, costly and politically unpopular. In the fields of technical research and scientific education, this attitude of technical supremacy, understanding the laws of science and the submission of nature, still prevails at all, including the very best, institutions of scientific education in the West.

In the field of human well-being, apart from welfare, there also has been a trend toward analytical, reductionist approaches. The anatomic dissection of the human body and the separate study of its components and their functions has led to an understanding of certain diseases and cures. Yet, this approach has led also to separate treatments of symptoms without considering fully the dynamic interactions between the organs themselves within the total organism, as well as the effects of mechanical or chemical human interventions from outside. In the beginning, this development had more beneficial than malignant effects. With the explosive growth of operational and pharmaceutical treatments, however, a dangerous imbalance is becoming apparent. As with industrial complexes, the microapproach is ignoring the macroeffect, this time not on the organism of the earth, but on the organism of the human being.

Awareness of disharmony sometimes leads to the observation that we should take nature as our model. The fallacy of this notion is that nature is not a model. We *are* nature. The split-up foundation of Western civilization has resulted in entrenched, structural and vested interests in industrial, social and political institutions. Education and religion have become subordinated to these institutions and, therefore, lack initiative and motivation for change.

Institutions are themselves locked up in their own specific survival codes, which sometimes results in their activities becoming counterproductive. They are following a track that leads to short-term results that are diametrically opposite to their long-term goals. Gary Coates describes this in an essay, ''Planning and the Paradox of Conscious Purpose.''[19]

The intuitive feeling of relatedness to nature is a fundamental vision that permeates Taoist thinking. The Chinese have no psychological problem with the fact that humanity is part of nature and consequently linked to the animal world. The Chinese have deep respect for nature. Throughout their history of thought, they have observed the processes and phenomena of the mineral, vegetable and animal world thoroughly and systematically. Theirs is not primarily a homocentric point of view. They observed nature from an aesthetic and holistic perspective, not taking things apart, but looking for the coherence and interrelatedness of single and collective appearances in nature. From this attitude stems the ancient method of acupuncture as a treatment of illnesses and bodily defects, as well as the use of herbs for curing the sick. Both approaches respect the wholeness of the organism and the organic whole of nature.

After A.D. 1000, the Chinese modified their philosophy by allowing themselves to accelerate the course of nature. This was done by extracting metals from ores and by intervention in organisms with artificial means. At this time in Chinese history, there were conflicting attitudes about these manipulations of nature in the interest of humanity. Such manipulation, however, was always thought of in terms of "theft."

This deviation from the original holistic principle is evident in the text written by a sixteenth century Chinese physician: "One cannot attribute events to fate. On the contrary man can act in such a way as to conquer nature!"[20] Nevertheless, acupuncture and herbs remain the major methods of healing in present day mainland China and, to a certain extent, in Taiwan. In both countries, in acute situations where these methods fail, however, recourse is sought to modern Western techniques. Conversely, acupuncture, herbal medicines and homeopathic healing are increasing in popularity in the West.

Teilhard emphasizes the unifying effect of collective knowledge generated by research and development at numerous places on earth and the growing density of technological exchange and mutual inspiration. He develops this vision in his "noosphere."

Teilhard's interpretation of the more or less linear scheme of evolution, as presented in Figure 2.2, made him concentrate his attention on the phase of collective consciousness of humanity. It is the increasing density of the noosphere that provides the foundation for a new leap. The mystical aspect of this road to progress and spirituality caused him to leave behind the preceding phases of evolution. His fascination with the dynamic movement of the universe in an irreversible direction, and the cultural code of his environment predisposed Teilhard to see all scientific and technological advances within the context of the emergence of human consciousness.

Teilhard became so caught up in the story of the human conquest of the natural world that he considered the artificial achievements of human technologies inherently superior to the spontaneous productions of the natural world. His focus on the decisive role of human progress in the present phase of evolution blinded him to the need to relate the new technologies to the total system of the earth.

Although Teilhard clearly saw the oneness of everything in the universe, including earth and humanity, he did not extend this integral vision to the role of technology. With respect to the progress of evolution, he inherited from his culture the sense of homocentricity.

Science and technology were, for Teilhard, only instruments to satisfy the need to advance beyond thresholds into the ultra-human. With this goal, he asserted that human intelligence should subordinate the natural world to human ends. Teilhard ignored, in this respect, humanity's interrelatedness with the earth, as an integral component of a functional biological community and of the larger earth process. Taoist philosophy is needed here to correct Teilhard.

The ecological side effects of technology and science through artificial transformations of nature were not apparent to Teilhard in his daily, practical life, nor were they part of his philosophy or concern. Although he recognized the dangers of plundering the earth, especially with regard to food production, he was very optimistic about technological solutions. He did not foresee that the very instrument of technology that could assist humanity in reaching a new phase in evolution could, at the same time, be the preventive cause through environmental damage.

The ultimate phase of evolution will never be reached if the planet is destroyed suddenly by nuclear war or through a gradual, but rapidly increasing process of life-destroying ecological disasters on a macroscale.

The Taoist approach towards nature needs to be revived world-wide if we are to prevent our own extinction.

## Oneness

We find the concept of oneness or wholeness in all philosophical and religious traditions of the world, going back to the ancient tribal origins and the ultimate Reality of Being, beyond the dimensions of space and time, the indescribable, with no name, totally transcendent. Although approached from different departure points, this notion can be recognized in Buddhism, Hinduism, Taoism, Sufi mysticism; in Plato and Plotinus; in Judaism and in Christian mysticism.

Bede Griffiths has pointed out that at this level of awareness no differences arise.[21] The question of how this notion or final state relates to today's world, however, is answered in fundamentally different ways. The Eastern religions and the Greek philosophers tend to approach the link more from a cosmic, psychological, spatial perspective, while the Judaeo-Christian tradition is oriented to a historical, personal and temporal concept, originating from the belief that Truth came to them through Christ. These two modes of experience are not necessarily opposed, but complementary.

The developments in the West that led away from oneness to distinctional and reductionist thinking have been discussed already. In the first half of the twentieth century, however, some remarkably creative breakthroughs have been achieved, specifically in the fields of physics and psychology. Physicist Albert Einstein and psychologist Carl Jung paved the way for new thinking. Both emphasized, in their fields, the interdependence of the parts of a whole and the relative value of isolating one factor in a system, without taking into account the interaction of that factor with other factors, including the observer. Interacting relations between factors, such as particles, waves, time, consciousness, unconsciousness, individuals and nature, were recognized as a new dimension in observing the world.

However, Einstein and Jung were still very much oriented to the spatial dimension and less to the temporal dimensions, at least not irreversible time. Einstein was trying to establish all the relations within the universe and was looking for a unified science of a total and final universe. He went so far as to call time an illusion[22] and was, in that respect, still basically a Newtonian. Jung was concerned with the interrelations between the individual human being and his or her environment, both conscious and unconscious, in present and past. He looked at it from a holistic, but reversible point of view. Irreversibility was foreign to both Einstein and Jung.

However, they took the important step to shift the emphasis from separate parts to whole systems. But they did not continue shifting from static concepts to dynamic, irreversible, evolving systems. We will return to this later, but the emphasis on whole systems led to new investigations and hypotheses in the macrodimensions of the universe, the biodimension of the human being and the microdimensions at the subatomic level. These developments, leading to new approaches in physics such as the relativity and the quantum theories, new field theories and new forces in addition to the traditional gravity and electromagnetic ones, revealed more and more the interdependence of everything existing. The great importance of relationships confirmed increasingly this interdependence, the awareness of the fact that relations between phenomena are predominantly shaping the phenomena themselves.

An additional new "discovery" of modern physics is that the position and functioning of any phenomenon in nature and within the universe not only relate to its near environment, but also to infinitely distant fields. This essentially means that everything in the universe relates to everything else in the universe. In the whole "web" of the universe, everything has presence everywhere. At the subatomic level, certain phenomena can be explained only through interaction with newly discovered fields at very great distances. These field forces are so weak that they are only becoming apparent at the microlevel. In daily life we do not notice these energies. This experience in new physics is particularly impressing the physicists who are directly and intimately confronted with these findings.

One of the latest contributions to this development is the hypothesis of "formative causation" by the British scientist Rupert Sheldrake. In simple words, he developed a theory and is in the process of proving that the code of forms or patterns of systems in any place in the universe is accessible to similar systems at any other place in the universe. New codes, once applied in sufficient numbers, become simultaneously accessible in the whole universe. In practical terms, this means, for instance, that once a new molecule and crystal is formed in a laboratory somewhere on earth, the formation of such a molecule and crystal in any other laboratory will proceed faster than the first experiment because the code or know-how is available

at any place in the universe. This is also called the morphogenetic field theory.[23]

The term for the interconnectedness of separate components of
a whole was introduced early this century by General Jan Smuts
of South Africa. In his writings on evolution and wholeness,
he coined the term "holistic." Dennis Gabor contributed to the
scientific validity of this concept through the development of the
holographic method.[24] New aspects of today's developments in
holistic thinking are the universal dimensions and the dynamic
element. This implies that the wholes themselves, including the
universe, are changing and unfolding. Even the laws of physics
are changing with this unfolding. A new contribution in this
respect is the science of thermodynamics of non-equilibrium
systems of Ilya Prigogine.[25]

Originally, this science was a technical concept in the field of
physical chemistry that won Prigogine the Nobel Prize in 1977.
Prigogine was intrigued, right from the beginning, by the philosophical and religious consequences of his findings if they were
of a universal nature.

The essence of his findings is that in a whole system there
is a creative potential that becomes increasingly evident when
the system is complex and far from equilibrium. Far from
equilibrium implies that the system is interacting heavily with
its environment to take in energy and matter. This is what
Prigogine calls the dissipative nature of the system. At a specific
moment in time, this system will show strong, strictly localized
fluctuations that can lead suddenly to revolutionary new configurations that are not related to the previous situation. Within
a short time, the whole system is subsequently transformed to
the new configuration. This phenomena also is called the self-
organizing principle of matter.

Erich Jantsch assumed this principle to be of a universal
nature in his book *The Self-Organizing Universe*.[26]

The important aspect of this development is a scientific
background for evidences of evolutionary dynamics of whole
systems, possibly including the universe. This is very close to
what Teilhard called cosmogenesis.

This self-organizing principle could explain leaps in the evolutionary process of the past and warrants the observation that
given the high degree of complexity and far-from-equilibrium
status of the human organism and the human society, conditions for new transformations are favorable. There is also a

link here with Teilhard's law of complexity/consciousness, be it more sophisticated and based on more knowledge than Teilhard could have at the time.

New visions of humanity, nature, universe, God and evolution are now coming from scientists like Prigogine and Sheldrake who work in fields closely connected with physics. They point out the philosophical and religious consequences of their observations and represent a new generation of spiritual thinkers who reunite once again the traditionally separate worlds of science, philosophy and religion.

Another category in Western society which presents a new dimension of universal interrelatedness is composed of psychologists, whose views on the wholeness of the individual and society converge more and more with the scientist's view on the universe.

There is a growing awareness of the presence of codes or stored information systems manifest in the individual and the cosmos. Codes start producing manifestations once the systems are activated by some selected form of energy. These information systems are present all the time and everywhere, but human beings (fortunately) do not notice all of them, because we do not yet have the ability to activate them. A simple example is the presence in the "noosphere" of the music of Bach, Bartok or the Beatles, but we only notice it when we set the radio dial at a certain frequency and feed energy into it. Then, suddenly, we hear a specific piece of music coming "out of nowhere."

It now is assumed that the universe is a total web of all codes. Maybe the universe as such should be considered as one basic code, of which all other codes are flexible and evolving subsystems. This is near to what David Bohm describes in *Wholeness and the Implicate Order*.[27]

In creative science, creative psychology and creative arts, the contribution to understanding evolution is the recognition and creation of codes, without "knowing" them. In this way, the universe is unfolding gradually, without indicating beforehand the moment and the direction of transformations, and yet within a basic harmonizing code. In the words of Barbara Hubbard, "the future is not predetermined but prepatterned."[28] The Taoists refer to the pattern or code of transformation as "li."

The "subcodes" of the existing physical components of the universe are chemically and genetically uniform and consistent, based on a select limited number of basic elements. They change slowly compared to noospheric changes. In psychology, the "coding" of the human being is not merely a genetic and physical formula, but also a mental and cultural formula, partially stemming from archetypical background and partially from fifteen to twenty years of individual confrontation with private and cultural surroundings.

Physicists are developing methods to better understand the universal coding, the individual's place in the universe and the possible fulfillment of his or her role therein. Psychologists are developing methods to understand our cultural and personal coding to match this fulfillment.

These methods, originating with Freud's analytical concepts and Jung's holistic concepts, led to gestalt, psychosynthesis and synergies with other methods. In essence, the psychologists guide the individual on the road of transformation at the micro-level, which in the context of the oneness of the universe, is directly connected with the macro-level and, therefore, in Teilhardian terms, with cosmogenesis.

The fundamental belief of the Taoist philosophers in the complete interdependence and reality of everything in the universe makes them unique in Eastern thinking. This is not the view in Buddhism or Hinduism. The Taoist vision is truly a cosmological approach where earth, humanity and cosmos are all important and interdependent parts of a whole.

Their conviction is that there is unity and order within the whole. This unity and order also can be found within the human being. "All things are already complete in oneself" is a clearly remarkable sentence from Mencius, 400 B.C.[29]

This also provides a background for the Taoists' opposition to covenants, legality and propriety, which they considered unnatural constructions from without.

According to Taoist thinking, every construction of a rule from without will lead automatically to the existence of the opposite, and thereby, the counterproductive interaction with the "rule" starts to work in human society. The notion of the Tao was already an important element in the *Book of Changes* (origin circa 3000 B.C.) and deeply rooted in all later Chinese thinking, as well as in Taoism and in Confucianism. It is, however, with respect to the rules of behavior that Taoist philosophy strongly opposes Confucianism. The Taoists believed in a natural universal code. By staying as close to nature as possible, one remains in tune with the code of the universe. By cultural codes which are transmitted through mental exchange from generation to generation, outside of the code-pattern of the natural, one runs the risk of conflicts within society and between society and nature, which, as Lao Tzu said, will lead to disorder.

Based on the assumption of a pattern, a unity, an existing harmony within the universe, the Taoist philosophers preached the doctrine of tranquility as expressed in chapter 48 of *Tao Te Ching* "by doing nothing, everything is done."[30] This last sentence is often ridiculed by people who operate in the middle of the bustling world where the action is. Sayings and texts by and on Lao Tzu and Chuang Tzu, though, make it very clear that they mean that one should do nothing against the pattern or natural Way which is the origin of the harmony model. However, it is sometimes necessary to use decisive and strong measures to prevent actions that would destroy the harmony of the natural Way. It is obvious that this only works where and when a human being has an undisturbed frame of mind, and can recognize and retain the universal code. It is clear that most people have not been very successful at attaining (or regaining) an undisturbed frame of mind. This has led to many deformations in human society and to the extensive presence of evil, what the Taoists call the "lost mind."

The notion of oneness and of a natural Way or code of the universe in Taoist thinking has a basic ontological orientation. Historically, it is connected with the idea of the "Golden Age," a mythological vision of a pure, unspoiled and harmonious world that existed in the deep past as can be found in chapter 39 of *Tao Te Ching*:

> In the remote past there were those who attained the One.
> Attaining the One, heaven became pure.
> Attaining the One, earth became peaceful.
> Attaining the One, God became spiritual.
> Attaining the One, the ocean became full.
> Attaining the One, ten thousand things came into life.
> Attaining the One, rulers became the models of the world.
> All of them became so through the One.[31]

In many cultures, this image of original purity plays an important role. It is comparable to the Christian concept of the paradise of Adam and Eve.

In Chinese thinking, the emphasis is on the backward journey of the human individual and society to this original purity, a code of oneness. In Christian thinking, the emphasis is on the forward journey to the Kingdom of God, based on a similar code of oneness.

The Christian notion of oneness was based on a fixed cosmos. The Chinese had more feeling for the dynamic, changing whole. Judeo-Christian thought emphasizes historical time within a fixed space and Indo-Hellennic thought emphasizes space with cyclical time. Taoist thought strongly sensed the interaction of matter, energy, time and space as a dynamic whole without emphasis. Because the Taoists did not have available the reservoir of twentieth century knowledge, they could not translate this sense into models such as those developed by Bohm, Sheldrake and Prigogine.

The *Book of Changes* (*I Ching*) was a model of the Chinese that resembles modern notions. It combines a systematic structure of sixty-four hexagrams, as a method to achieve access to the code of the universe, with chance (the unpredictable factor) and change (the dynamic factor). It reveals a picture, a manifestation, of one's individual position at a moment in time, connected with the past and the future within the context of the oneness of everything.

It is this aspect of Chinese thinking that so much impressed Carl Jung. He had developed his theories on the importance of the unconscious, both individual and collective, and its relationship to the ancient past. He saw the link with the universe in the unconscious element in the human being. He believed in the interconnectedness of simultaneous events without a direct cause-effect relation: the principle of synchronicity. In other words, he believed in universal fields that connect events in time and space where normally one would speak of "coincidence." Feeling quite isolated with these new, partly mystic concepts within a hostile professional environment, Jung was delighted to find fundamentally similar notions in the *I Ching* and in Taoist philosophy. He describes this encounter in his introduction to *The Secret of the Golden Flower*, a Taoist text on life and meditation.[32]

In the thirteenth century, the view on oneness in Chinese thinking was refined further by the scholar Chu Hsi, the architect of neo-Confucianism.[33] The essence of this philosophy was that there exist two major factors governing the course of events in the universe: a universal pattern or principle, or as they called it, the "grain of jade," characterized by li, and the force of energy, psychic and physical, which is the motor of development, characterized by Ch'i.

Chu Hsi's approach provided a synthesis of Taoist, Confucian and Buddhist thinking and an impulse to a broader scope of oneness in Chinese culture.

In *The Divine Milieu* and other essays Teilhard makes his conviction clear that he sees human functioning within the cosmogenetic context.[34] He bases this partly on his belief that the divine is within the individual who is part of earth; earth is part of the universe and the universe if part of the divine. Teilhard also was impressed by the increasing, collective and emerging awareness, through discoveries by science, of a more vast and organic One. He also derived his conviction through intuition. He emphasizes that, in Christian belief, the human being has the capacity to "see" the oneness and does not only have to "know."

The dynamics of the transformation process through which earth, humanity and universe are progressing—a notion only potentially present in the Chinese thinking—gave Teilhard inspiration to suppose a coherent process within a total system. He expresses this in yet another way by postulating that the universe is a single psychic system. In *The Phenomenon of Man*, he writes "The stuff of the universe, woven in a single piece according to one and the same system, but never repeating itself from one point to another, represents a single figure. Structurally, it forms a Whole."[35] Each element of the cosmos is positively woven from all the others. Although in his time he did not have access to the latest findings in subatomic physics and the morphogenetic fields concept of Sheldrake, the self-organizing principle of Prigogine, or the implicate order of Bohm, Teilhard is stating in a few words what we have encountered in the scientific findings of today. Teilhard translated his convictions and feelings on oneness in his concept of the Divine Milieu, the milieu that is within us and surrounds us everywhere in the physical and metaphysical world.

Although in Teilhard's thought the emphasis is on the wholeness of the universe as we perceive it today (its totality) and a projection into the future (its becoming) where humanity and the universe will complete the wholeness in the pleroma, he also alludes to the origin of the wholeness in the past: "Traced as far as possible in the directions of their origins, the last fibres of the human aggregate are lost to view and are merged in our eyes with the very stuff of the universe."[36] Teilhard emphasizes that in order to understand and see the wholeness or oneness of the universe, the human being must study and experience the mysteries of matter. For the earthly human being, matter is the key to the concept of oneness. Without matter we have no existence on earth. This viewpoint is treated comprehensively in *The Heart of the Matter* and complements his treatment of the subject in *The Divine Milieu*.

Taoist and Teilhardian thinking have a parallel sense of oneness as both believe in the all permeating unity in past, present and future. There is a similarity in the Taoists' description of the Way, the Tao, and Teilhard's picture of the Divine Milieu, ever-present in and around the human being, nature and the universe. Both recognize the actual and participative involvement of the human being and earth in the cosmic process. Both are world-affirming.

# Change

"From the Tao, one is created,
From one, two,
From two, three,
From three, ten thousand things.
All of them achieve harmony through the unification of affirmation
and negation
Which is embraced by everything."[1]

The element of change has profoundly in-
trigued and occupied the minds of human beings through the
ages and has had a great impact on their worldview. The following analysis shows some of these views and the Taoist and
Teilhardian thinking. In the first section, the general awareness
of change in the sense of transformation is discussed. In the
second section, the element of time in the process of change is
described, and in the third section, a survey is made of how the
notions of change in time and form are translated into religious
concepts.

## Transformation

The dynamic and creative unfolding aspect of the universe as
described in the previous chapter (Teilhard's cosmogenesis) implies constant change. Change in the sense of movement from
one situation to a new one and from one form or shape into a
new one is an important element in both Taoist and Teilhardian
thinking.

In traditional Christian thinking, the separate and independent creation by God of the earth and all its living species has
always been an important doctrine. We still find strong defen-
ders of this notion today in the creationists who oppose the
teaching of only evolutionary theories at schools.

In the nineteenth century, in a later development of the mechanistic worldview, Darwin postulated his theory of the origin of species. In the beginning of the nineteenth century, he traveled for years as a young botanist with the sailing ship *Beagle* around unexplored coasts and islands in South America and the Far East. He studied intensively the flora and fauna of these remote areas. He came to the conclusion that the various species he had observed were differing in sometimes minute and sometimes major aspects as a result of varying environments. These differences could occur at isolated places, independently and without cross–fertilization.

After more than twenty years of gathering and analyzing evidence, he finally published his *On the Origin of Species* in 1859.[2] He could not sustain his policy of postponement because he became aware of a similar publication being prepared by Alfred Russel Wallace who had studied this phenomenon in Malaya.

The essence of Darwin's thesis was that emerging shapes, colors and functioning of species in the living world were selected as a result of surrounding conditions and were transferred, as adaptions, through procreation. In short, species are not fixed and separately created at one moment in time by God. Darwin did not speculate on the mechanism by which new forms emerged, nor did he extrapolate into the past or the future. As a scientist, he deliberately avoided the speculative word evolution! Others used this term after him.

Darwin's theory created a completely new thinking in the Western world about nature and humanity. There was great opposition to the idea that, as an ultimate consequence of Darwin's theories, the human could have descended from the animal world, through a process of transformations. It was bad enough to discover that humanity and the earth were not the center of the universe, as postulated by Copernicus and Galileo in the sixteenth century; the possibility that the human being was a highly developed animal was seriously disturbing to Christian thinking. This problem was directly related to the doctrine of the radical distinction between the human and the natural world. Of course, it was fascinating for the mechanistic thinkers that with the theory on the selection of species a mechanism was discovered in the natural world. Opponents claimed that there would never have been time enough for all the supposed transformations because, according to the interpretation of scriptures, the earth was created in 4004 B.C. However, in the middle of the nineteenth century geologist Charles Lyell had shown that the age of our planet must be billions of years.[3] Presently it is estimated at 4.5 billion years.

Paleontological and biogenetic discoveries in the twentieth century increasingly reveal data that make theories of evolution acceptable. The theory of "the survival of the fittest" (as a species in the prevailing environment, not, as often thought, in fighting other species), a term that was not used by Darwin, but originates with Spencer in the second half of the nineteenth century, is now expanded with sophisticated theories on the mechanism of the emergence of new forms, the mutations. Mutations are changes in the building blocks of genetic material that are responsible for transfer of characteristic properties in living species from generation to generation. These mutations can be caused by external influence, such as radiation and chemicals. They also can occur spontaneously. Scientists and biologists worked out chance mutation theories at the genetic level within cells and theories on selective mutations and "self-organizing" mutations.

The progression in the theories is the result of the awareness that chance is not the only factor in these changes. There are internal or implicate patterns and sophisticated forces at work. Through these forces, especially the self–organizing ones, major transformations can take place in short time intervals. This seems the answer on the observations from creationists' quarters, that fundamental leaps such as the original development of the eye cannot be explained by chance and adaptation. Observations in physical chemistry reveal that the forces and the pattern show a strong element of intentionality. The most up-to-date theories of evolution of Prigogine reveal that the higher the level of complexity and the degree of nonequilibrium in the evolving system,[4] the more likely these self–organizing mutations are to occur. The higher the complexity and the farther away from equilibrium, the more conditioned the system is for an unpredictable radical transformation to a new and different order.

The origin of the phenomenon of transformation remains a mystery. Western civilization, through science, has learned a great deal, however, about the mechanisms of transformation. This knowledge has been applied in such areas as the chemical industry, the pharmaceutical industry, the food industry and genetic engineering. In these fields, we have taken transformation into our own hands; but we do not know the origin of the phenomenon, nor take into account the universal interacting dynamics of change. These dynamics imply that transformations are never isolated processes, but are directly linked to both the immediate and distant environments. There are, therefore, great risks on this road of artificial transformations by humanity. The long-term consequences of radical interferences with the natural pattern can be far-reaching.

Transformation is an essential element in Taoist thinking. The continuous transformation of all things and situations is the fundamental basis of the *Book of Changes* (*I Ching*), which precedes Taoist thinking, yet contains the element of the Tao and the alternating yin-yang principle of duality in unity.[5] Although in Chinese thinking the principle of eternal return is dominant, there are also elements of a sequential order and uniqueness of events. The sequence in chapter 42 of *Tao Te Ching*, contains an element of linear time. This is confirmed by the notion that all manifestations have a unique character. Their strong intuition with regard to the interconnectedness of the unique parts of the universe and nature implies the principle of unity in diversity. These observations indicate that transformation in Chinese thought contains evolutionary aspects. Transformation in the evolutionary sense was implicitly conceived by Chuang Tzu in his description of the transformation of species. He states that humanity is rooted in the originative process of nature. "All things come from the originative process of nature and return to the originative process of nature."[6] Chuang Tzu describes the mechanism of adaption to various environments. He was aware of a process, although still in principle a cyclical one.

Taoist philosophers, from 300 B.C. to A.D. 1400, pay considerable attention to organic development, metamorphosis, zoological transformation, repeated evolution and speciation. They observe improvements in successive stages and levels of nature as well as of human society. Taoists firmly denied the fixity of biological species. An important aspect of their approach is that there were no religious doctrines or scientific conceptions that would have impeded their intuitive, spontaneous and holistic thinking in these matters. Transformation in the classical Chinese sense was the way for everything, living and nonliving, to obtain its correct nature and destiny (called *ming* by Lao Tzu) and would result in great harmony. The Taoists regarded every moment in the transformation process as unique and the process itself as linked to a pattern throughout the universe.

The young Taoist philosopher Wang Pi (A.D. 225–249) in his commentary on Lao Tzu integrated the idea of the universal principle, called 'li', that underlies all changes and transformations.⁷ Wang Pi preferred this concept over 'ming' or 'destiny'. In the various Taoist and later Taoist-related philosophies, the moving force of the transformation is the 'Ch'i,' an energy within the substance. The 'li' principle, combined with 'Ch'i,' is remarkably similar to today's concept of the self-organizing forces mentioned above. The combination of 'li' and 'Ch'i' was to become a major element in the later development of neo-Confucianism by Chu Hsi, as mentioned earlier.

When Teilhard was five years old, his mother was cutting his hair near the fireplace. A lock of hair fell in the fire, darkened and disappeared, upsetting him totally. For the first time in his life he knew he was perishable. Perhaps his mother said something like: "Pierre, do not cry. Things do not disappear, they transform."

Transformation is a central element in Teilhard's thought. Evolutionary transformations from energy to matter, from matter to life, from life to consciousness and from consciousness to self-consciousness are parts of a transformation process involving the universe, our planet and human being. Teilhard could describe this process in a much more refined and detailed manner than Chuang Tzu did because of the vast amount of information that had become available through profound scientific and philosophical developments and achievements through the ages.

This last aspect of collective and documented experience which increases so rapidly, especially in the twentieth century, made Teilhard believe that self-conscious human beings are building up a more and more concentrated reservoir of factual information and spiritual awareness resulting in a global consciousness. He called this new dimension the "noosphere" (from the Greek word *noos*, meaning mind), an evolutionary phase in the sequence of the emerging of the geosphere (the earth) and the biosphere (the living world). This is illustrated in Figure 2.1. He considered the noosphere an important dynamic element of cosmogenesis. According to Teilhard, the rapidly condensing noosphere will form the medium for the intensive continuation of the process of transformation, at the level of the human species.

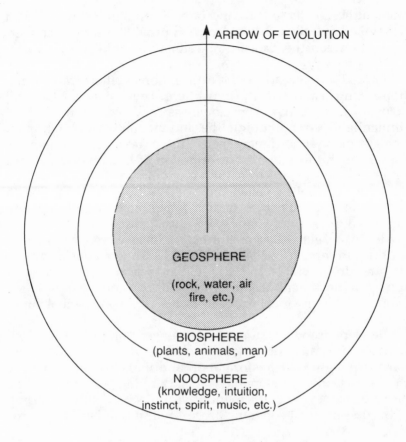

FIGURE 2.1 Evolution of Planet Earth through geosphere and biosphere to noosphere.

In the whole process, he assumes the moving force to be basically a cosmic psychic energy. In the next section, there will be more information on his vision of this process. The essence is that Teilhard, as shown in his early essays, already was convinced that creative transformation is an ongoing process, that there is no fixity of species, and that in the course of time fundamental changes take place that are of a unique character and are part of a cosmological movement, within a coherent pattern and with a distinct and a linear direction. In this last respect he differs with the Chinese view that is more inclined to a circular movement of unique events. The ambiguous nature of this notion leads intellectually to the concept of a spiral or a cone, an idea developed by Teilhard.[8] This concept provides room for convergence between the Taoist and Teilhardian thinking on transformation.

Teilhard's view leads to the expectation of a new transformation arising in and from the noosphere. This transformation will lead to a collective consciousness and common soul of humankind, strengthening the individuality of the human being, union without merger. In this context, Teilhard expects that through this major transformation of humankind the end point of evolutionary transformations on earth finally will be achieved in what he called the "omega point." According to his vision, this coincides with the biblical expectation of the Parousia, the second coming of Jesus Christ.

Although Teilhard's transformation ideas were embedded in a Christian context, the Roman Catholic Church considered his theories unacceptable. In 1924, Teilhard was requested to sign a retracting document on the "materialistic" and "panpsychic" aspects of his theories, exposed in his essay on original sin in 1922.

The element of transformation was very important for Teilhard's vision, and critical for his relation with his Church. Teilhard's thought on transformation and its key to evolutionary thinking clearly complements Taoist thinking, adding scientific and religious experiences to intuitive and scarce understanding of the presence of an ongoing process within a universal context.

## Time, Direction and Progress

An important issue that has intrigued human beings in all cultures, religions and ages is the notion of time.

Originally, time was connected with cycles of day and night and with the cycles of the seasons. The movements of the moon, the sun, the planets and the earth in relation to the stars led to further definitions of time spans; yet time remained limited and cyclical. Until and including the age of Plato and Aristotle, the notions of a cyclical, ever-returning course of events held sway. Distinct from the daily, monthly and annual cycles, other cycles varied according to the phenomenon observed, wherein all the phenomena would return and the returns were eternal. Human cycles, as well as the individual's particular past and future, were related to timeless mythological gods, goddesses and heroic archetypes who provided guidance and protection during life and after death.

In the West, this notion of cyclical time changed fundamentally with the Christian religion's concept of the historical arrival of Jesus Christ, Son and incarnation of God, at a specific moment in time, a so-called one-time event.

Christian religion became a main source of consistent historistic thinking. This thinking involved irreversible directional development and was not cyclical. The idea of developmental time with one-time events, with direction and irreversibility originates with the New Testament story of the life of Christ. The birth of Jesus Christ, His death, the resurrection and His future return are such one-time events.

Consciously and unconsciously, the emergence of this interpretation of time—developmental time superimposed on cyclical time—has become a cornerstone of Western civilization. Jesus Christ is not only a timeless mythological guide and protector, but a real man, sent by God, on a certain date at a certain place here on earth. We speak of B.C. and A.D. Historicity, this in itself is not new or relevant because other civilizations, for instance the Chinese, also connect time definitions to events. Today the Chinese year zero corresponds to A.D. 1911, with the proclamation of the Republic.

A great difference is that the Chinese have started again and again with a new time "box," while in Western Christian thinking, time is a duration with interconnected, sequential and continuous developments that eventually will lead to paradise, the final "box" of Pandora! *Et tunc erit finis.*

The historical and developmental time concept does not exclude the transcendental and mystical aspects of the myth of Jesus Christ, the examples of purity and the link between the human individual and the divine. The symbolic and poetic dimensions in the biblical story have a meaning that reaches different levels of awareness than historical facts and future expectations do.

However, the progressive, evolving concept of time has induced in Western thought a linear, goal-orientated life-style. For many people, this attitude has resulted in "the end justifies the means" philosophy, and has contributed to a shift of emphasis from inner awareness of the dynamic present to an image of outer and future goals in life.

The inner awareness of the personal and global evolutive present is an indispensable source of energy for a meaningful public life. Unalloyed outer and future thinking alienates the human being from functioning naturally.

The more the subject is analyzed by cerebral methods, the more inconclusive the results. Using reason, we can explain that we never "are," because every moment which we want to "fix" as "being" becomes instantaneously the past. We cannot grasp the present because it has gone before we can get hold of it. If we cannot contemplate the present in its fullness, we can only reflect on the past and think of the future, but we never really "are". Some philosophers, including Teilhard, therefore describe everything as in the state of "becoming," a positive and evolutionary thought. The mental difficulty of this approach is of the same nature as in the example where we could not intellectually grasp the moment Achilles overtakes the turtle.

The implication of modern physics for our concept of time is that time is relative, although not reversible. We need new definitions of different notions of time. Henri Bergson, with his concept of duration being different from deterministic time, and Prigogine, with his distinction between durational, irreversible Time (T) and mathematically reversible time (t), have made attempts in this direction. The concept of entropy, a property of thermodynamic systems, that leads a closed system on an irreversible road to eventual disintegration and chaos, is closely related to the notion of irreversible time. Until very recently, this phenomenon was reason for scientists and some philosophers to assume that this would also be the fate of the closed-system universe. Prigogine has shown that the self-organizing forces of far-from-equilibrium systems have the capability of intensively dissipating energy and matter, and thereby, can more than compensate the entropy effect.

Let us now leave the realm of philosophy and science and come back to the question in the introduction: "Who am I and what (on earth) am I doing here?" What we really are worrying about, in our Western linear thought process is: "Am I coming from somewhere and am I going somewhere?" The developmental time concept in Christianity, during nearly two thousand years of living with this concept, has fixed us Westerners in linear thinking.

And yet, this sense of direction in developmental time has stimulated Western humanity to investigate processes in nature and to develop theories of evolution. Charles Lyell's demonstration of the vast geological time span and Charles Darwin's demonstration of the development of species, in the nineteenth century, greatly contributed to evolutionary thinking. For Darwin, this was not an ideological or religious question. He stayed purely within the context of the scientific method and his profession. Darwin did not speculate on, nor want to have anything to do with evolutionary theories about the future of humanity. Karl Marx asked Darwin to write an introduction to *Das Kapital*, because Marx saw a direct link between Darwin's analysis of the development of the past and Marx's own historic-materialistic vision on the social evolution of human society. Darwin refused because he wanted to retain his scientific objectivity.

Nevertheless, evolutionary thinking expanded. Major visionary contributions came from France, from Bergson, Lecomte du Nouy and Teilhard de Chardin. Many advances have been made in the last fifty years in the fields of paleontology, geology and genetics. These advances increasingly provide evidence of the correctness of the concept of evolution. The Roman Catholic Church has opened its doors for careful recognition of a development of this kind in the Pastoral Constitution "Gaudium et Spes" of the Second Vatican Oecumenic Council in 1965, inspired by John XXIII.[9] The encyclical "Humani Generis" by Pius XII in 1950, still mostly rejected this line of thinking, implicitly attacking Teilhardian thought.[10]

The slow progress in acceptance of evolutionary thought is illustrated in the United States, where teaching religion in public schools is forbidden by the Constitution. Strong protests are made by Christian fundamentalists (or creationists) because only the theory of evolution is being taught in these schools. They claim that creationist arguments also should be heard. Nevertheless, it seems that in the Western world, the principle of evolution has become widely accepted, except officially by the Roman Church, and is becoming an important factor in the way we think about the future. Implicit in evolutionary thinking is the irreversibility of change and the clear distinction from the idea of cyclical and eternal returns. This has also led to the typical Western focus on "progress." Progress, though, is narrowly defined as an increase in knowledge, well-being and welfare of humankind.

The Western world has reached a high degree of saturation, even supersaturation, of materialistic progress. At the same time, contemporary physics and psychology are revealing new aspects of the interrelatedness of time, space, energy and matter, consciousness and unconsciousness. We also have learned more about the holistic nature of the universe, earth and humanity. The combination of oversaturated human progress and awareness of the organic nature of our planet, leads to a review of our limited, homocentric concept of progress. In the evolutionary sense, progress refers to the whole of nature. The burning question is whether human progress in its present stage is not counteractive to the progress of the whole natural world. It is becoming clear to many people in the West that the moment for re-evaluation of our ideas on time, direction, and progress has arrived, because regress on the planetary level also means regress on the human level.

Time has always been an important aspect of Chinese life. The Chinese view time as basically cyclical, but of a very sophisticated nature. They were active in the writing of history, more so, and much earlier than the Europeans. Chinese historians counted years in terms of dynasties and reigns. They worked out a coherent "single track" or sequential theory of dynastic legitimacy and tried to correlate the chronology of events.

As time went on, there grew up various forms of history which continued through various dynasties. This pattern was set by the earliest historian, the brilliant Ssuma Chien (A.D. 100). He wrote the first general history of China beginning with the remotest antiquity and continuing up to 100 B.C.[11] Although the Chinese years were contained in compartmental "boxes," interconnections were made, and later historians added to the sequential records.

The Chinese used calendars as early as 700 B.C. and were the first to have clock systems. They also worked out methods to estimate the time spans of great cycles, derived from celestial movements, and from the *Book of Changes* (*I Ching*). The cycles had ranges of a hundred thousand years, and the "great cycles" a hundred million years or more, comparable to the cycles of the Greeks and Buddhists. These cycles were of such enormous magnitude that there was no incentive to worry about a before or an after. Just as they felt no need for "a creator," they did not feel the need to further investigate or analyze cosmic time.

The Chinese model of time is neither the arrow nor the circle. Similar to the mystical undifferentiated notion of the Tao, the

Chinese had an undifferentiated notion of cosmic time. It has been described as "a placid, silent pool within which ripples come and go."[12] The expression for "the universe," *yu-chou*, essentially means space-time. In other words, the awareness of a continuum of time and space, formulated by Einstein, was intuitively present in the old Chinese philosophy.

From about 400 B.C. definitions can be found of duration, space, movement and time, that come very near to our present knowledge in modern physics. That the Chinese were aware of a direction in time is clear from their motivation and their fostering of progress. They experienced an increase of knowledge about natural resources, and a sequence of discoveries of ores and subsequent metals. There was an increase in the application of knowledge in such fields as alchemy, hydraulics, civil engineering, mechanical engineering, the compass for navigation, explosives and book printing. They meticulously studied nature, the behavior of insects, plants and animals. They observed transformations and developed a primitive notion of evolutionary process.

The historical development of Chinese civilization included the Confucian doctrine of social morality, as well as the necessary measures to develop order and improve the social structure of human society. The Chinese were aware of the element of change. This is shown in *The Book of Changes* (*I Ching*), which originated more than three thousand years ago. It was amended, expanded and commented upon by many sages, the most important being Confucius. The *I Ching*'s theme is "Change, that is the only thing in the universe which is unchanging."[13] A central concept is that every instant is of a nonrecurring, unique nature.

Another principle of the *I Ching* is that it connects thoughts, events and actions that have no apparent causal relation, but are occurring simultaneously. This is a notion similar to the principle of synchronicity developed in the twentieth century by Carl Jung. Jung refers frequently to the *I Ching* in a special essay on this subject "*Synchronicity: An Acausal Connecting Principle*".[14]

These examples show that the Chinese capability of combining cyclical, linear, holistic, irreversible, directional, mystical and rational thinking in one total, universal concept of life was remarkably advanced. Western civilization has struggled for two thousand years, taking everything apart and then connecting everything together again.

Joseph Needham has written on time and knowledge in China and the West:

> Enough has surely now been said to demonstrate conclusively that the culture of China manifested a very sensitive consciousness of time. The Chinese did not live in a timeless dream, fixed in meditation upon the numinous world. On the contrary, history was for them perhaps more real and vital than for any other comparably ancient people; and whether they conceived time to contain a perennial fall from ancient perfection, or to pass in cycles of glory and catastrophy, or to testify to a slow but inevitable evolution and progress, time for them brought real and fundamental change. [15]

In 1940, Teilhard finished his manuscript *The Phenomenon of Man*. This book, after publication in 1955, gave a sudden impetus to public awareness of his message that the universe is engaged in cosmogenesis, an unfolding process of expansion and renewal, and within this process our planet and humanity are evolving, irreversibly and directionally with a purpose and pattern, through the activation of consciousness.

He based his evolutionary thinking on the increasing evidence that, in the history of the universe, new phenomena emerge in a continuous process of increasing complexity, culminating at present in the most complex and most unified phenomenon of organisms: the human being.

A schematic presentation of evolutionary phenomena is shown in Figure 2.2.

Teilhard's conclusion from these phenomena was that, with increasing complexity of the configurations formed during evolution, hidden potentials of internal energies (psychic energies) are released. This process leads to subsequent emergence of life, consciousness, individual self-reflexive consciousness and collective consciousness. This is Teilhard's principle of complexity-consciousness. According to his view, the most recent phase in the development of the human mind is the discovery of evolution.

The element of developmental time is a crucial aspect in his concept of evolution. In the schematic presentation, several one-time or unique events are indicated. These events are characterized by the emergence of a new phenomenon that manifests itself at one moment in time. The new phenomenon introduces a new form of complexity, a new center of orientation and coordination. This new form provides the basis for further development in quality and growth, until a new saturation point

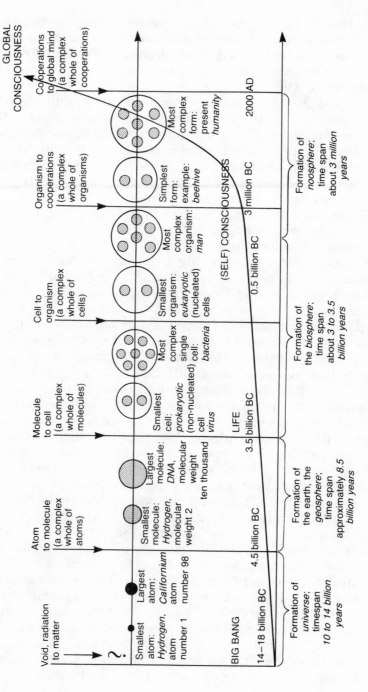

FIGURE 2.2  Diagram of Evolution.

The arrows indicate a moment of transformation, discontinuity, leap or a one-time event.

is reached that will again lead to a transformation to a higher level of organization, configuration and coordination, and so on. In this way, the atoms precede the molecules, which lead to the cell, the organism, the human being and human society with many stages in between.

Teilhard extends his phenomenon analysis with an extrapolation into the future. He expects another one-time event to happen during the further development of the human community. In the future, a new saturation point in complexity could be reached through the noosphere, where evolution will reach an end point. Teilhard called this the omega point. At this point, humanity would achieve the Kingdom of God, the full realization of the mystical body of Christ, the union of individual and collective consciousness and the end of time.

Teilhard describes this evolutionary process as a cosmic process, a cosmic evolution which transcends local temporal processes on our planet in an unfolding universe. The active and increasingly decisive influence of human self-consciousness is of central importance in this process of evolution. The human species as such has not developed further physically for three or four hundred thousand years, except in size of population. However, human mental and intellectual capabilities have bypassed the traditional process and contributed to a new type of evolution. Eyesight has been extended by microscopes, telescopes and television into the micro- and macroworld. Memory has been extended through libraries and computers. Knowledge has been extended by collective information and teamwork in all fields of science. Hearing has been extended by mechanical devices that can pick up sounds at the subatomic level as well as deep in the universe. Capacity of musical appreciation and reproduction has been extended by stereophonic recordings. Movement has been extended to travel through space. Conversely, the contemporary person is partly losing the ability to depend on the natural senses.

The new type of evolution takes place in an exponential pattern. The nature of an exponential growth curve is shown in Figure 2.3. The examples mentioned have contributed to a communication explosion whereby practically all events and facts can be known simultaneously in all corners of the world, within a "web" of signals in a vibrating layer enveloping the whole earth.

Teilhard called this the noosphere and felt it was rapidly increasing in density, growing to an ever greater state of complexity, and leading to a new leap in evolution.

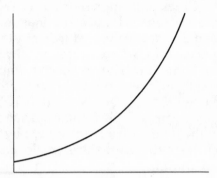

FIGURE 2.3   An exponential curve.

The role of the individual and humanity is decisive in this process. Humanity has taken transformation into its own hands by transforming natural resources, natural life, energy and the elements: water, air and earth. Humanity now has the capacity either to destroy our planet totally or to create a new phase in the process of cosmogenesis. Teilhard's great contribution is to make humanity aware of the gigantic dynamic process that has been unfolding irreversibly since the beginning of the cosmos. Teilhard notes the unique element that the human being, with its super-complex nervous system, constitutes in this process. He also describes the influential role humanity is assuming at this point in the history of the universe.

Teilhard developed his concept as a consequence of his experience in his paleolontological field work. The more he worked it out, the more he became involved in its philosophical, religious and mystical implications. As he was clearly a man of Western culture, it seems that the religious, philosophical and anthropocentric codes of this culture led to his creative visions. On the other hand, however, they may have inhibited him in reaching a radically new, total concept that would have resulted in a truly universal and new cosmic story, without ambiguity.

### God and Creation, Beginning and End

The basic doctrine of Western Christian thinking is the existence of a transcendental, personal God who governs creation. This doctrine is based on the belief that the universe as a whole must

have a cause. The Greek philosophers Plato and Aristotle described God as original cause. Thomas Aquinas in the thirteenth
century developed this causal theory further by taking examples
from the observable world, where causes are always found to be
ordered in series. Something causing itself is impossible. "One
is therefore forced to suppose some first cause, to which every-
one gives the name God."[16] This is a rational approach.

The question of the supposedly infinite old age of the universe
was not dealt with. A remarkable statement by St. Augustine
(fourth century) that "the world was made, not in time, but
simultaneously with time"[17] was not taken into account in the
development of the doctrines.

In the age of Aristotle, the universe as a whole was considered
fixed in that all movements and changes within the universe
were cyclical, guarded by God and ever-returning. In the seventeenth century, Newton, Descartes and Laplace developed the
notion that God initiated motion and that from that moment on
everything became mathematically calculable, measurable and
predictable. Through the ages, many inventions and discoveries
have challenged the traditional religious doctrine of God and the
Creation. The basic doctrines Thomas Aquinas reformulated on
request by the Pope in the thirteenth century, however, have
remained, in the Catholic Church, the unshakable foundation of
Christian thinking. The clashes of the Church with Galileo,
Newton, Darwin and Teilhard are illustrative of the gap that
developed later between religion and science on the subject of
Creation and God, as a consequence of the rigid doctrines.

It was, and still is, an essential shortcoming of the leaders of
the Church that they have not been able to reconcile new
scientific findings with Christian belief. Rejecting and ignoring
the evolutionary evidence leads to an increasingly inadequate
and unrealistic approach to the world's problems. In recent
years, the subject of creation again has become a controversial
topic, because of the consequences of the latest discoveries in
subatomic physics and physical theories about the origin of the
universe. Fortunately, there are quite a number of physicists
who now publish reasonably understandable books on the subject, such as Paul Davies' *God and the New Physics*. The essence of
their findings is that the cause-effect principle does not apply at
the subatomic level and, therefore, is no longer a universal principle, as was assumed in Aquinas' causal theory. Secondly,
neither the infinite nor eternal age of the earth, nor the theory of

a creation *in* time are compatible with holistic, nonlinear concepts. The intuition of St. Augustine is increasingly confirmed: time appeared simultaneously with our universe.

We cannot visualize what this really means because our urge to think of a beginning and an end is intimately related to the limited dimensions of our short stay on earth. In the past, the mystics argued that other fields, other dimensions and other patterns are present outside of our limited world of observations. Now physicists and mathematicians, the last to be suspected of mysticism, tell us the same story.

It was Teilhard who predicted this in 1924, in *Mon Univers*.[18] The discussion in the West regarding God, Creation, beginning and end centers mainly on a supposed controversy between creationists and evolutionists. This discussion appears to be more and more futile, because while religion should be able to accept certain facts (such as nonfixity of species and the law of complexity consciousness) without in any way touching the religious and divine principles, science is in a position to accept mystical and one-time event phenomena without disturbing the professional principles. In fact, there is no fundamental difference between the concept of creation and the self-organizing principle.

Early Taoist writings did not mention a personal God in the sense that we conceive of Him in the West. The Tao was the notion of an origin that was neither being nor nonbeing, nothing one can describe or define, not connected with anything and at the same time connected with everything. The Tao as origin did not require any further analysis. It was sufficient to accept the notion of the Tao, leading to One, (in neo-Confucianism: *Tai Chi*), leading to Two, Three and the Ten Thousand Things. Although the Tao is basically a notion of interconnectedness, outside the dimensions of time and space, its manifestation implies a certain sequence, but without a cause-effect relationship.

A. C. Graham has described recently the difference between the conceptualizations of the underlying ground in Chinese and Western thought. "The goal which Western philosophy has pursued has been the Reality beyond appearances on the assumptions that once we know the Truth about the cosmos we shall know how to live in it. Taoists do not think in terms of discovering Truth or Reality."[19] They indicate a notion by using stories, verses, aphorisms and all available sources of art to express their intuitive feeling about the Tao, the Way by which to live and to die. A typical example is found in chapter 51 of the *Tao Te Ching*:

Tao creates all things,
Te cultivates them.
Things are shaped according to their natures,
Relational conditions fulfill them.
Therefore, ten thousand things all venerate the source of Tao
And value the potentialities of Te.
Tao is venerated and Te is valued spontaneously,
No one orders that it be so.[20]

The strong Taoist belief in the interconnectedness of everything present, past and future made the Taoists philosophically indifferent to cause-effect observations. This is an astounding intuition, going far deeper than the intellectual struggle through confusion and doubt that characterized Greek and Christian thinking. Again, it must be emphasized that the spirit of analysis and conflict in Western thinking led to active search and innovative thinking. The natural and unity-based spirit of Chinese philosophy led to holistic contemplation and, in some way, to nonaction and resignation.

The Chinese felt no need for one personalized God who governed creation. They believed in creative forces within the universe, within nature and within the human mind. The foundation of their belief is the Tao, which manifests itself in the universe, and yet, is beyond the universe. The notion of Tao is near the notion of God. The notion of Tao, however, never is conceptualized; it just is.

Teilhard's work gives evidence of his strong belief in basic Christian doctrines, his commitment to his Church and to his order. The dogma of God as personal creator and Jesus Christ as divine incarnation are, for Teilhard, so vital that he is not able to adapt them. He was not yet familiar with the latest developments in physics, although he must have sensed them. However, neither basic Taoist philosophy nor the new discoveries in physics sufficiently penetrated his thinking to the extent that he chose to re-evaluate the interpretation of the Christian story.

Teilhard made observations that connect his thought with Taoism and modern physics. Examples are: "the divine or universal milieu," "the kingdom of God within us," or "God is infinitely near and dispersed everywhere"; "all realities converge upon the ultimate point"; "our minds are incapable of grasping reality without our being compelled by the very structure of things to go back to the first source of its perfections."[21] It seems as if he comes very near to the notion of Tao, but he ultimately contains his intuition within the Christian context.

The coinciding of Teilhard and Taoist thinking can be visualized partly by comparing their approach of the "ultimate point." For Taoism, this is the One, the T'ai Chi from which everything originates. For Teilhard, this is the omega point toward which everything is converging. In Teilhardian terms, Taoism is alpha-oriented and Teilhard is omega-oriented. For Taoism, before alpha there is Tao; for Teilhard, after omega there is the Kingdom of God. Although they have somewhat different views on the elements of time and space, we can sense a symmetry in their visions of the ultimate reality.

Marie Ina Bergeron draws attention in *La Chine et Teilhard* to the coincidence of the Taoist and neo-Confucianist concepts with those of Teilhard.[22] A simplified visual presentation of the symmetry can look like this:

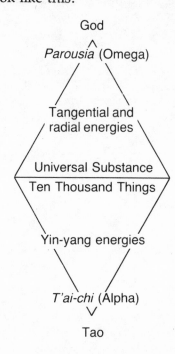

The image suggests that we look at alpha and omega as complementary opposites within the context of oneness and interconnectedness. We can recognize the concept of unity in diversity in the upside and the downside cone.

Within the context of his loyalty to Christian belief, Teilhard had innovative concepts on the separate creation of the species, the relations between matter and spirit, the principle of evil and the relation between humanity and divinity.

He expands the dimensions of the human perspective on the world by including the infinitely small, infinitely large, infinitely complex, and the cosmogenetic process that we are part of and which includes all these dimensions. Teilhard reveals the mechanisms of evolution and universal principles of nature such as the consciousness/complexity relationship. He has the strong mystical feeling of the oneness of the universe and its manifestations. In this aspect he was near to Taoism and modern physics. On the subject of a personal God and creation and the fundamental doctrines of Christianity, however, he is very distant from the Taoist viewpoints. Much of the distance is not a consequence of different fundaments, but different cultural conceptualizations.

# Human Values

"Can you unify hun and p'o into one and not let them be
   divided?
Can you concentrate on your breathing to reach harmony and
   become as an innocent babe?
Can you clean the dark mirror within yourself
   and let nothing remain there?
Can you love the people and govern the state
   and do so without interference?
Can you enter and leave the realm of Non-being and let these
   actions take place by themselves?
Can the clear illumination radiate to all directions without your
   having knowledge of it?
Cultivate it, and nourish it,
Produce it, but do not posses it.
Labor on it, but do not depend on it.
Lead it, but do not manage it.
This is called the mystic attainment."[1]

Philosophical and religious contemplations
on distinctional or unified worldviews and on the essence of
change obviously have not only influenced societies as a whole,
but also the individual human being. The following sections
demonstrate the effect this had on human values and the
specific thoughts that Taoists and Teilhard developed in this
area. The first section investigates the thinking on the personal
human identity and immortality. Later sections describe how
value systems in human society are related to the nature of the
worldview as it developed through the ages.

## Individual Identity, Life and Death

In all civilizations, the existence of the individual human soul
and the phenomenon of life and death have always been a matter

of considerable concern. Speculation about the preexistence and immortality of the individual also occupied the minds of Greek and Christian philosophers.

Without going into the details of the various theories, assumptions, myths and doctrines, we may reasonably conclude that there is no rational answer to this question. Christian belief asserts that God has created every individual human being separately and in God's image. After death, the soul survives, is judged, and may enter the Kingdom of God, where souls keep their individuality as part of a higher form of collectivity.

In atheist circles, the human being, body and soul only exists here and now. Before and after life, there is nothing.

In the Western world, there is not much choice between these two viewpoints. The subject of life and death preoccupies many people, but is suppressed because it is an uncomfortable theme with unsatisfactory answers. Usually it flurries up when there is direct confrontation with great suffering or dying, but subsides if and when normal life resumes. The temporary focus on the mysterious and frightening events of illness or death passes, even if it leaves a mark.

Both believers and nonbelievers now are entering a new dimension of thought due to the increased sophistication of evolutionary theories and new findings in science and psychology.

The individual is confronted with the factual and mystical experiences of universal interdependence, of the interconnectedness of all phenomena, of the relativity of time and space, and last but not least, but relativity of outer appearances and the experience of inner forces through meditation. These experiences lead the individual to develop an inner sensitivity to the uniqueness of personal being and to discover relationships outside the physical body and physical environment.

This development in consciousness breaks away from traditional and conventional patterns and still encounters resistance in the world of facts and figures. This new awareness transcends linear, external and nihilistic doctrines. It opens the road of transformation to a more mature and cosmic approach to the essence of individuality which goes beyond life and death on the planetary level.

Taoist philosophers were not concerned primarily with identity before or after death, since the earlier philosophers considered personal identity an illusion.

"My birth and my death are no more than moments in the universal process of transformation," writes Chuang Tzu.[2] He considered:

> the liberation from selfhood as a triumph over death and that not personal consciousness will survive death, but in losing selfhood one shall remain what at bottom one always was, identical with everything conscious or unconscious in the universe.

Chapter 16 of *Tao Te Ching* puts it this way:

> Things are unceasingly moving and restless,
> Yet each one is proceeding back to the origin.
> Proceeding back to the origin is quiescence.
> To be in quiescence is to return to the destiny of being.
> The destiny of being is reality.
> To understand reality is to be enlightened.
> Not to understand it, and act wrongly, leads to disaster.
> Reality is all-embracing.
> To be all-embracing is to be selfless.
> To be selfless is to be all-pervading.
> To be all-pervading is to be transcendent.
> To be transcendent is to attain Tao.
> To attain Tao is to be everlasting.
> Even when the body dies, it is not the end.[3]

and in chapter 33:

> To know others is to be intelligent.
> To be aware of one's self is to be awakened.
> To overcome others is to have superior strength.
> To overcome one's self is to be vigorous.
> To be satisfied is to be wealthy.
> To act with power is to be aspiring.
> To retain one's source is to be long-lasting.
> To die yet not to be deceased is to have longevity.[4]

Here we touch upon the fundamental viewpoint in Chinese philosophy: our pure and unspoiled and unique individuality is to be found in our origin. After we are exposed to the outside world, we become aware of our bodies and our surroundings; we build up an image, obtain names and status and become part of the "ten thousand things." We develop selfhood and become attached to our external images, our personal identities. The Taoist philosophy of life moves from external to internal reality. Chapter 48 of the *Tao Te Ching* expresses this as follows:

in the pursuit of learning, every day something is acquired
in the pursuit of Tao, every day something is dropped.[5]

In this process, the individual transcends through the barrier of
the opposites to the pure inner self. From Chuang Tzu, one can
deduct that in the Chinese mind the "real" individual has
always been there and will always remain, what "at bottom he
always was."[6]

In the *Huai Nan Tzu* (circa 100 B.C.) a more specific interpretation is given with statements such as:

> Metamorphosis connected with physical death does not change the
> essence of man;
> The imperishable responds by corresponding with the changes of
> the perishable; such a process is indefinite;
> That which causes living does not die; that which has been caused to
> live dies; that which causes transformation is not transformed; only
> the transformed being is being transformed.[7]

In Chinese thinking, these principles of transformation apply
to the microcosmos of the individual as well as to the macrocosmos of the collectivity. The transformations of microcosm and
macrocosm are interconnected and interdependent.

In later developments of Taoist thinking, especially in the
religious and mystical interpretations, there is a curious shift
from a nonattached approach to immortality to a strong emphasis on "longevity," or long life on earth. Here the desire for
transcendent immortality overlaps the world-affirmative
nature of Taoism.

Teilhard's vision is similar to the Taoist notion of the ultimate
unity as it exists within the individual. And yet, Teilhard stayed
close to the Christian traditions concerning individuality in that
he consistently emphasizes the continuity of personal identity
after death. Teilhard's approach is much more person-oriented
and remains connected with the total concept of body and soul.
This conforms with the Christian doctrine, where on the day of
the Judgment and arrival of the Kingdom of God all the dead
will resurrect.

Teilhard was critical of the Eastern view that human individuality ought to become submerged in the vast ocean of
collective spirituality. For him, maintaining the total human
within the context of the collective consciousness at the omega

point was essential; one should be united while remaining one-self, converge without fusing.

As discussed earlier, Teilhard saw the individual's development during his or her lifetime, as a shift from active involvement in earthy occupations, contributing to the evolution of the planet, to the more divine connection with and contemplation of the spiritual world. Attachment and diminishment were not mutually exclusive in human life. There is a parallel here with the Taoist approach. Yet, views on the preservation of the personal identity after death differ. Both Teilhard and Taoism link the individual directly to the supreme ultimate (God and Tao). Teihard's approach embraces the personal and the spiritual; Taoism emphasizes the pure spiritual. For Teilhard, the Creator has a personal image; in Taoism the supreme ultimate is not personal.

## Good, Evil and Love

Western culture had developed in the last two thousand years under the shadow of historical, Original Sin or the Fall and the inherent evilness of humankind. This powerful doctrine of Christian belief has had a substantial influence on the diminishment of feeling for organic relations between the human and the natural world. It meant that Western thinking accepted that there was a historical and structural conflict within reality, conceived as opposite forces. The conflict had to be resolved by a conquest of good over evil, of light over darkness.

In the same context, the Christian belief held a dogmatic approach to human sexual relationships. Sex was meant for procreation only, not for the experience of the interaction and all the mysterious and affectionate aspects that go with it. This private aspect was taught as part of the inheritance of Original Sin or the Fall of humanity. These assumptions have contributed to the conflict model that dominates the Western world. This model accepts conflicting duality as the basic building block of human society; only through crisis and conquest do new syntheses emerge in an ever-evolving process.

The highly innovative progress of the Western world is a positive consequence of this philosophy of transformation through crisis. This concept also formed the basis of the dialectic theories of Hegel in the nineteenth century, whose theme was: thesis and antithesis lead to synthesis. In Hegel's system, ultimate knowledge would be achieved after many stages of this dialectic speculative process.

In each stage, previous thinking is integrated into and surpassed by a higher level of development and systemization. This gives Hegel's thinking the character of elevations, leading to the absolute truth and the elimination of evil. This approach advanced modern thinking along the course it had chosen since the mechanistic viewpoint started to prevail.

Western philosopher Martin Heidegger opened up a radically opposite line of thinking that comes near to the Taoist approach in his *On Time and Being*. According to Heidegger's view, Hegel will only arrive at a metaphysical concept of reality or truth. The essence of reality, according to Heidegger, is not reached through a process to a concept, but through awakening of the inner self; not through elevation, but through "going back." By going back, one reaches forgetfulness of all evil and all good, and one's inner potentiality identifies with the higher reality.[8]

The Christian viewpoint is that the destination of humankind will be reached in redemption and salvation. This can be considered as a solution that had to be invented to make up for the man-made concept of historical sin. The individual has to follow certain moral codes and will be judged at the day of redemption, with the risk of going to hell instead of heaven. In the twentieth century, such an approach, even if symbolic, is no longer adequate to inspire the individual to find an acceptable level of creative fulfillment in life.

It is within the context of confrontations and sinfulness that the subject of love lost its original spontaneity at the human level in Western thinking. Love, however, is the manifestation of one of the most pronounced and mysterious forces in the cosmos: attraction. Forces of attraction are universally present in the microcosmos (elementary particles) and macrocosmos (stars and planets). Love at the human level is an inspirational manifestation of the universal phenomenon of creative attraction. Without creative and dynamic attractions, the universe would not exist.

In Eastern philosophies and related religions, as well as in the Islamic religion of later date (sixth century A.D.), there is a complete absence of the notion of original moral and historical sin. This holds also for Taoist thinking.[9]

As the Taoist philosophy is based on original and ultimate

unity, there is no place for structural evil. Out of unity emerge complementary opposite manifestations: male/female, heaven/earth, dark/light, day/night, happy/sad, life/death, high/low, difficult/easy, long/short, being/non-being, front/back, valley/mountain, weak/strong.

These manifestations exist by the grace of their opposites and interact all the time. In Chinese thought, they are of the yin yang type of opposition which is ultimately more complementary than contradictory. Chapter 2 of *Tao Te Ching* illustrates this:

> When beauty is universally affirmed as beauty, therein is
> ugliness.
> When goodness is universally affirmed as goodness, therein is
> evil.
> Therefore: being and non-being are mutally posited in their
> emergence.
> Difficult and easy are mutually posited in their
> complementariness.
> Long and short are mutually posited in their positions.
> High and low are mutually posited in their contradiction.
> Voice and tone are mutually posited in their unity.
> Front and back are mutually posited in their succession. [10]

Evil only exists because good exists. If there were no evil, there would be no notion of good. Evil, denoted by Taoist thought as the "lost mind," will disappear when the distinction disappears as a result of ultimate unity and harmony within the inner self of the human being. Therefore, the Taoists do not accept external measures, confrontations, conquest, rules and laws, but emphasize "nonaction" through individual following of the natural Way, subsuming opposites through constructive instead of destructive attitudes. In chapter 62 of the *Tao Te Ching* it says "Even if a man is unworthy, Tao will not exclude him." [11]

Early Taoist writers devote little discussion to the subject of love, in the general sense, the specific individual sense or in the sense of sexual relationships. In chapter 67 of the *Tao Te Ching*, Lao Tzu mentions love as one of the treasures of the Tao [12] and presumably means the universal love of interaction and affection. Regarding specific love between individuals, it must have been assumed as being a natural manifestation of the universal phenomenon. The world-affirming attitude of the Taoists, with their positive interpretation of the human earthy existence in all its interconnections with nature and the universe, considered the sexual relationship a natural event in human life. The microcosm of human sexuality is parallel to the notion of the yin yang as both are complementary opposites interacting in union. There is no trace of the Western kind of approach to this subject. In later Taoist thought, sexual energies are considered important intermediates to develop psychic energies necessary for going back to internal harmony. In reaching the stage of the ultimate reality and attaining Tao, the male/female distinction and the sexual aspect disappear.

Teilhard considered evil as a developmental aspect of the creation, although in a different sense than the Taoists. For him, it was a part of the process of growth, trial and error, the evolution of the world, and individual development through life on earth. Especially in *Le Milieu Divin* and *Human Energy*, Teilhard describes this vision and uses the term "transfiguration" when describing the evil or painful aspects of life by integrating them in a plan of improvement. "Everything evil is capable of becoming good."[13] Essential for this transformation is the belief and trust in God, in the ultimate divine.

Teilhard has incorrectly been criticized for ignoring the evil aspects in this world. He devotes considerable attention to the subject in his writings, including an appendix in *The Phenomenon of Man*. As a result of his experiences as stretcher-bearer in the First World War and in the face of the atom bomb over Hiroshima, he was very much aware of the dreadfully ugly aspects of the present world. In the final pages of *Le Milieu Divin*, however, Teilhard expresses his belief that, although he accepts the existence of hell as a structural element of the universe, "the damned are not excluded from the Pleroma," the ultimate redemption. This is similar to the earlier quoted sentence in chapter 62 of *Tao Te Ching*: "Even if a man is unworthy, Tao will never exclude him."

Teilhard also says:

> "the fires of hell and the fires of heaven are not two different forces, but contrary manifestations of the same energy; in the ultimate divine milieu there is unity."[14]

In other words, Teilhard recognized, experienced and accepted evil as part of the process of differentiation and ultimate union, a view that was similar to the Taoist concept of duality and unity. Teilhard and Taoism are basically optimistic about the eventual disappearance of evil in the human venture.

Universal love is of central importance in all Teilhard's works. It is the driving force, the psychic energy inspiring humanity to new dimensions of consciousness and the enrichment of the noosphere. For him, love means the taste or zest for life, the universal form of attraction, the relation to the ultimate Divine, the completion of individualization between man and woman, and charity toward one's fellow beings.

We see here once more his unifying vision on earthly and divine phenomena, micro- and macroaspects of the same milieu. For him, evil is an unavoidable aspect of progressive evolution. Love is the force that urges us forward and draws us upward.

Both Taoism and Teilhard have views on the subjects of good, evil and love that are more constructive and inspiring than the attitudes Western civilization has developed.

## Female and Male

It is common knowledge that the notion of male supremacy entered Western and Chinese civilization at an early stage. The female was clearly the basis for stability, continuity and creativity in early civilizations, but in the subsequent division of tasks in the emerging communities, as described by Bertrand Russell in *Marriage and Morals*, the male became the dominant member of the family and later in society.[15] This transition from matriarchy to patriarchy happened worldwide.

Unnatural and contrived divisions into female and male have now penetrated so deeply into the cultures of the world that they dominate social structures and human behavior. As a consequence, sexual role hierarchies create uncooperative and inefficient labor as well as lack of creative individual fulfillment.

In Western civilization, this development was supported by the male-oriented Christian tradition, from Adam, through Abraham and Moses, through Jesus and the Pope, to our Father in heaven. In China, the strong male orientation of the teachings of Confucius contributed to this emphasis.

Taoist thinking, on the other hand, is based on a dynamic, balanced harmony of the female and male aspects of nature. There is a notion of a primordial female origin, from which male and female aspects differentiated. This can be found in *Tao Te Ching*.

Chapter 6:

> The Spirit of the Valley never dies.
> It is called the Mystic Female.
> The Door of the Mystic Female
> Is the root of Heaven and Earth.
>
> Continuously, continuously,
> It seems to remain.
> Draw upon it
> And it serves you with ease.[16]

Chapter 28:

> He who is aware of the Male
> But keeps to the Female
>   Becomes the ravine of the world.
> Being the ravine of the world,
>   He has the original character which is not cut up,
> And returns again to the (innocence of the) babe.[17]

Chapter 52:

> There was a beginning of the universe
>   Which may be regarded as the Mother of the Universe.
> From the Mother, we may know her sons.
>   After knowing the sons, keep to the Mother.
>   Thus one's whole life may be preserved from harm.[18]

In *The Spirit of the Valley*, Sukie Colegrave has studied and described extensively Taoist philosophy's appreciation of the female nature of the origin and of the male/female aspects of nature including the human being. Her study of androgyny offers substantial support that Taoist views can shed new light on the unnatural process of radical sexual distinctions human societies have developed over the ages.[19]

According to Taoists, the yin (female) and yang (male) manifestations in all aspects of nature are interchanging, exchanging and complementary opposites. Yin and yang also exist within the human being, man or woman. This last observation is crucial, as the absence or loss of this notion is the reason that in our present world a man must perform according to his male image and suppress, always and at all cost, the female element that is psychologically and genetically an intrinsic part of his being. In this respect, there is a connection between the theories of Carl Jung and Chinese philosophy. The unconscious male aspect in the female, which Jung called the *animus*, and the unconscious female aspect in the male, which he called *anima*, have an affiliation with the yin-yang principle of interchanging complementary opposites. Also, Jung's concept of a personal and a collective male/female unconsciousness is paralleled by Chinese thinking: *hun* (male, personal, spirit soul) and *p'o* (female, personal, earth soul), *hsing* (human nature, male, logos) and *ming* (human life, female, eros).

Jung regained these notions by going back into the mythological and unconscious realms of human beings, where he uncovered Taoist similarities.

In *Human Energy* and *The Heart of Matter*, Teilhard expresses his strong feelings about the feminine aspect of nature and specifically the human being. He speaks of the necessary synthesis of the two principles, male and female, in the building of the human personality. The masculine can only escape from isolation through the awakening of the feminine, through which the wholeness of the world and the interconnectedness of everything can be sensitized. He calls this the complete human molecule that is already around us, a more synthesized element and more spiritualized than the individual personality. It is a duality comprising masculine and feminine together, according to Teilhard.

Teilhard believes the union of the two elements in a person can be accomplished through intensive interaction between female and male individuals. Eventually this will lead to a higher level of completeness for each, a transformation to a new human being, a step to a new humanity. Teilhard, like Taoism, emphasizes the feminine as the origin and basis of the universal process. His intuition on the function of the feminine, much influenced by his personal experience, brings him to the belief that the unifying cement in human society and future development of humanity is the Universal Feminine.[20] Teilhard's approach comes very near to Sukie Colegrave's concepts, and this illustrates the parallels in Taoist and Teilhardian thinking.

As we become aware of basic harmony and the interdependence of all events and elements in the universe and on our planet, the issue of the primacy of the male in our cultural code is subject to fundamental revision. The Taoists' and Teilhard's unifying visions on the female and male aspects of nature can help us to reestablish the balance of these mutually complementary manifestations of creation, to the benefit of the future of humanity.

## Art

In essays or books on philosophy, science and religion, the subject of art is seldom treated. Yet, art has always been an important medium to transmit the cultural, religious and philosophical ideas and concepts of the world.

Chinese art reveals the fundamental Chinese outlook on life. Recently many observers have studied this relationship.[21] Ancient and contemporary paintings and sculptures depict the element of changing opposites, an underlying continuous pattern, and the wholeness of the natural world. A human being, when part of the picture, is typically a small and integrative element in the totality of the work of art.

Western art includes numerous works with an emphasis on nature. In general, though, the personal and homocentric elements that are so central in Western philosophical and religious attitudes, are much more pronounced.

Chinese calligraphy, a less descriptive but more transcendental art form, indicates a sense or impression of a reality behind the physical or psychological experiences and appearances in actual life. The Chinese sense of relativity and their notion of direct, dynamic interdependence with the Tao are expressed in art and in their artistic way of writing. As is typical of Chinese culture, the two arts painting and writing, were taught and applied in combination—a holistic approach. The images or ideograms in their written language leave ample room for interpretation and avoid clear-cut rationality. Many civilizations at some stage of their development changed from hieroglyphics to a linear alphabetical system, but Chinese characters (and to a lesser extent the Japanese) have remained basically the same from the ancient past to the present day. The written Chinese language does not cut up mental thoughts and impressions into a linear sequence of separate words. Typically written communication has many more expressions than does oral language.

In the Western world, modern art increasingly tends toward a holistic notion, opening new frontiers of expression that are still closed to conventional linear and reductionist styles of its social, industrial and educational systems. Art in the West should be seen as an important medium for advancing new and evolutionary awareness in Western thinking.

Confucius considered music to be the foundation of general

education. He was so impressed by music that he isolated himself from society for some years so he could learn to perform it himself. "Music is related to goodness; by making music one obtains a good, righteous and natural heart."[22] On the other hand, Mo Tzu was of the opinion that "making music kept farmers and merchants from their fruitful labor and led to higher tax burdens for the people if the ruling class was surrendering to musical distraction."[23] This viewpoint was shared by Rousseau in the eighteenth century.

Teilhard de Chardin was never very impressed by music. He enjoyed Fauré occasionally and did not dislike music, but it did not really interest nor affect him. He only once deals briefly with the role of art in liberating human psychic energy.[24]

Generally speaking, music is mentioned very seldom in ancient and modern philosophical works dealing with human destiny. This is surprising because music contributes great joy of being on earth. It gives us an intense feeling of connectedness with the universe, the ultimate divine and the mystery of life. What is a more subtle union of matter and spirit, of tangible and intangible, of mechanical and spiritual, of interior potential and exterior forms than the musical instrument, the musician and the music produced? Musical instruments have unlimited potential to transmit feelings and moods, mystical experiences, and a sense of relatedness to transcendental dimensions of consciousness. Music is a unique spiritual medium that emerges from a rare combination of high technology, wood or metal, specialized techniques and emotion, transcendence and love.

Out of this creative combination comes one of the most spiritual, holistic, harmonious and mentally stimulating experiences of life. As an example, the highly mathematical, harmonious, cyclical, yet intuitive, romantic and mystical elements in the partitas and sonatas for solo violin and the suites for solo cello by Johann Sebastian Bach achieve a profound ultimate unity that reminds one of the essence of Taoist thinking. These musical expressions were created by a man who lived in the seventeenth century, in the midst of a strong movement toward a mechanistic worldview.

This original and inspiring achievement of the reunion of the divine and human world can be experienced in the music of the composers with whom one feels a particular affection. The experience of musical art, and many other arts, is very near to original and ultimate unity. The arts preserve, in their own cultural code, the message of intuition and spontaneity that is the basis of Taoist thinking. During the so-called Age of Reason, Western civilization could have lost this intuitive spontaneity. The arts, however, continued and continue still to play an essential role in the reunion of humanity and nature, of body and soul. They inspire harmony within the human soul and provide a model of universal harmony as well. Therefore, it is essential to transformational processes in human society that the human individual participate in artistic expression.

CHAPTER

# 4

# Conclusions from the Comparison

The visions of Taoism and Teilhard can be of great interest for the development and maturation of Western thought. When their visions are combined, they present an even stronger case, either by mutual reinforcement when they converge, or by complementary values when they diverge.

The following summary lists a selected number of observations where Western thinking and Taoist and Teilhardian visions present new challenges. They indicate the areas where Western thought can benefit from the inspiring ideas of Taoism and Teilhard.

- The world we live in is an integral part of the total system of earth, humanity and universe. The human being is part of nature and part of the universe. Through life on earth, the human being participates in a universal pattern. This vision is world-affirmative.

- The total system of the earth, humanity and the universe is in a continuous process of creative unfolding. Transformations are leaps to new levels of interconnectedness, creating unique events and manifestations. There is no fixity of species.

- Universal psychic energy is the all-pervading force that creates spirit and matter, soul and body, energy and force, mind and universe. There is a pattern and an intentionality in these manifestations of psychic energy. The manifestations are different forms of the same substance.

- All manifestations have dualistic characters. This dualism originates from unity and returns to unity. The interchange and transformation of dualistic and different qualities within a pattern of unity is at the core of a dynamic creative process.

- The process of change produces diversity in union. There is a constant interplay between the uniqueness of the individual part and its confirmation within a unifying whole.

- There is a continuous relationship between the micro- and the macroelements in the universe. For integrative evolutionary actions, this relationship is of vital importance. Both the concept of unity and the concept of process depend on this notion.

- In the context of process and progress, Teilhard emphasizes directional time and Taoism cyclical time, but both views contain elements of each. The notion of coherence of past, present and future in Taoism, which corresponds to the whole circle image, and the notion of the primacy of the future in Teilhard's work, which corresponds to the linear arrow image, can be reconciled symbolically in the image of the spiral or the cone. The cone or spiral manifests the coherence of the whole and has an additional dimension: to escape from the finite dimension of the circle.

- The coherence of the past, present and future in the context of the evolution of the earth is a factor in the reconciliation of Teilhard's emphasis on the human's predominant role in the noosphere phase of evolution with Taoist emphasis on nature as a whole. Noosphere, geosphere and biosphere are integral parts of the total evolutionary process. Specifically with respect to science and technology, Taoism's strong belief in the wholeness of nature complements Teilhard's belief in homocentric progress through the noosphere.

- Taoism's belief in the continuity of the individual essence and Teilhard's belief in the immortality of the personal identity, as well as the Taoist belief in an impersonal Tao and Teilhard's belief in a personal God, result from their emphasis on nature and on humanity respectively. The Taoist biocentric view complements the more homocentric thinking in Western culture.

- The development of the individual and humanity is embedded in an environment of infinite time, space and creative universal energy: *The Divine Milieu*, and the Way or Tao.

- During life, a mature human being shifts emphasis from external to internal orientations, from earth/spirit to universe/soul. In the process, he or she develops more and more harmony and reaches unity between individual and ultimate reality.

- The ultimate relationship between individuals and the Divine or the Tao is that they are all part of each other and mutually present in each other. Therefore, there is fundamental unity.

- Love is the force or energy of attraction and affection that has universal scope and presence. Love between humans is a micromanifestation of a macrophenonomenon. Love is a treasure and a driving force in evolution.

- Evil is an unavoidable aspect of differentiation out of unity, of the notion of progress and creation. Sacrifices are indispensable in the creative process. Evil will be resolved in reaching or rejoining unity.

- Female and male manifestations are implicit in the process of differentiation out of the psychic energy. Differentiation into male and female originates from unity and returns to unity. During life on earth, the human being will seek internal and external harmony between these two complementary and equal aspects of nature.

- Artistic experiences inspire harmony within the human soul and provide access to universal patterns of unity. Art plays an essential role in transformational processes towards dynamic individual harmony.

- Harmony within the individual, following the natural Way, *The Divine Milieu*, will lead to harmony in humanity, which in turn will lead to the rediscovery of cosmic unity and subsequently the rediscovery of nature and peace.

The Taoists were less pressed for time, two thousand five hundred years ago, with regard to the survival of the earth. Taoist contemplative wisdom and Teilhard's awareness of creative evolution, however, form a valuable combination that can guide us today, when we have less time for survival.

# Part Two

Applying the Views of the Taoists and Teilhard de Chardin in Today's World

# Emerging Worldview

Reading, thinking, listening and living gradually lead the human individual to develop a concept of what life is all about. Expressing this completely in words is not possible. In this respect, Lao Tzu has the following comment in chapter I of the *Tao Te Ching*.

> The Tao (Way) that can be told of
> is not the eternal Tao;
> The name that can be named
> is not the eternal name.
> Nameless, it is the origin of Heaven and Earth;
> Nameless, it is the mother of all things.
> Always nonexistent,
> that we may apprehend its inner secret
> Always existent,
> That we may discern its outer manifestations
> These two are the same;
> Only as they manifest themselves they receive different names.
> That they are the same is the mystery
> Mystery of all mysteries
> The door of all subtleties.[1]

Nevertheless, an attempt is made in the following paragraphs to present some formulations. These formulations are subjective and will be interpreted somewhat differently by each reader, because of individual and cultural codes that will select, emphasize and interpret according to particular taste.

Everything we experience, learn, and expect is part of a story, a story we consciously or unconsciously believe in and which fascinates us. This story and its pattern cause us to make plans, to create ideas and to participate in life. Its beauty and meaning give us inspiration, courage and zest. Today, the magnitude, coincidence and intensity of changes around us make many people ready for a new story.

*Where do we come from and where are we going?* The universe, as we experience it, is itself a manifestation of a dimensionless, infinite and timeless void. In this void, everything existing and nonexisting is potentially present. This notion is beyond our intellectual and practical sense of understanding. We can only get a "feel" for it by absorbing and digesting what we hear, see and sense in our surroundings, our heart, our dreams and our subconsciousness.

We know now that much more information and many more interrelations are present in the universe than we can see, hear or formulate with our limited physical and intellectual capabilities. We may conclude that the universe itself originates from the void, but we cannot grasp the meaning of the void.

Assuming that the code of every manifestation of the void and of the universe is universally present, my conclusion is that the code of the manifestation of the individual human was, is and will always be. The individual code of genetic and spiritual identity or soul becomes manifest at the moment of individual physical conception on this earth; it will return through the universe to the void at the moment of physical death. Individual identity can become manifest again out of the union with the void. Our bodies, minds and external images as well as our works on earth become part of our total being, as part of the universe, during the manifestation of our personal identities on this planet. When we die, these will return to the collective physical and mental environment that, for the time being, is present in, on and around our planet: the geosphere, the biosphere and the noosphere. They will be part of the evolutionary cosmogenetic process.

*Is there a beginning and an end?* The concept of the void and, successively, the universe, our planet and humanity, implies a historical time element. We experience change and transformation in a succession of stages within the universe that we now estimate to have taken eighteen billion years to evolve. This number of years is part of the time box in which our thinking takes place. Within that time box, there is a beginning and there will be an end. It does not imply an absolute beginning or an absolute end, because the universe is a manifestation of the void, which is dimensionless, timeless and infinite. Within the manifestations of universe, planet and humanity we cannot understand this, but we can accept it because we do understand that, conversely, the manifestations are themselves parts of a higher order of existence, the seamless web of the universe.

Within our time box, the universe, the planet and humanity are irreversibly developing, and progressing in a pattern. From the moment the universe came into existence out of the indistinct unity of the void, there has been growth, in quantity and in quality. There also have been cycles of creation and decay of species, and of integration and disintegration.

On the whole, since the universe came into existence, there has been evolutionary progress. Progress is meant in the sense of Teilhard's phenomena (see Figure 2.2). The fundamental key to this progress is the principle of complexity/consciousness. In the process, humanity is becoming aware of evolution, through self-consciousness. This consciousness is progressing exponentially to a higher level of global, collective consciousness. Collective human consciousness is increasing rapidly in density and quality and moves toward universal consciousness, a seamless web. Humanity is becoming increasingly aware of and part of this universal consciousness and is, through new physics, receiving signals about forces and fields in the universe that are directly related to life and evolution on earth.

The end of our time box will be reached when human, global and universal consciousness become one. This event, called the omega point by Teilhard, is not an absolute end, but the threshold of a new and unknown field. If we consider the factual data of the evolution of our planet and the growth curves of all its manifestations, it is not unrealistic to assume that this threshold could be reached within fifty years. This will be explained in the next chapter.

***What about Creation and God?*** The insights humanity has developed in the last decade support the universal interrelatedness of all manifestations. The discoveries of new laws and fields surpass but contain the previous physical, chemical and mathematical concepts. With this development of consciousness, humanity now is able to understand the essence of "oneness," the fundamental force that is moving us, adding a new dimension to our awareness.

The intuitive, spiritual and mystical elements in all the world's religions sustain the notion of oneness. This pure vision is found in Christian, Jewish, Buddhist, Hinduist, Islamic or Taoist "stories" of creation and destiny. The proliferation of dogmas, traditions and differentiation of the religions has distorted somewhat the original awareness of oneness and resulted in the present variety of interpretations and contrasts between dominating religious empires.

The ancient and renewed awareness of oneness and mystery sustain the belief in a relationship of the individual to a higher order of existence. This higher order of existence is what is meant by words like God, Tao or Brahman. More essential than words is the awareness of the relationship. This relationship can be found in feelings, dreams, meditations and revelations. It is individually conditioned and can be recognized by many individuals within the specific religious traditions.

*What Are We Doing Here?* We are comforted by the thought that our individual identities, our individual codes, our vibrations are in union with the universe past, present and future. The question remains: What is our function during this passage on earth, what motivates us, and how do our lives fit within the evolutionary process we are experiencing in and around us?

Conscious human beings have the opportunity to think about or act on these issues. Many human beings die before they reach awareness of their role in evolution, because they die in infancy, in misery or in mental deficiency. These human beings have their relationship with the higher order of existence just as any other human being does. Their manifestation in this world has been impeded by physical or mental defects or mechanical accidents. These external aspects do not take away from their unique individual identities.

The concept of being part of the universe and part of the planet implies that the human being is not a separate isolated creation, but an intricate "mode" within the total system. As such, we are not observers or outsiders in the evolutionary process. We play an active role within an individual and collective process. Religious language would translate this conscious role of humanity as the fulfillment of a divine pattern.

In the course of evolution, the human being has become the most complex and subtle organism that exists within the immensity of the observable universe. Self-consciousness enables the consciously participating human being to make decisions and to choose between options that are beyond the capability of other living organisms who are acting and reacting mostly according to instinctual patterns. Human power or responsibility is a two-sided coin, however. Our manifestations in the universe are subject to defects, aberrations from oneness, imperfections and chance. Evolutionary imperfections have been mistaken for human sin.

Manifestations in the universe have dualistic properties that are seemingly contradictory, but basically complementary and always interacting. Dualism has confused the human being since the time of transformation from tribal to reflective life, about three thousand years ago. The confusion of dualism has led to alienation from the natural processes within which humanity is such an involved partner. It led to the assumptions of two different worlds—the spiritual and the earthly—and this led to a belief that it is necessary to choose between the two, mutually exclusive worlds.

Humanity must redefine its role on earth, so as to be in and of the earth, part of the creative and active completion of the earth in the process of evolution. This inclusive attitude can be sustained by an awareness of the harmonies of the geosphere, biosphere and noosphere. With this comprehensive awareness, the human being will find an acceptable level of fulfillment. Of course, one can ask the questions: Why has humankind this function? What happens if it does not fulfill its mission?

In this respect, the story of redemption, final judgment and the idea of punishment related to our behavior no longer seems adequate. I think the relationship with the higher order is far too subtle and integrative for such a "human" approach. It seems that the answer to the questions above is that we instinctively and intuitively follow the way to the union of human, global and universal consciousness. Individually we reach this union in death; during life we can reach it through spontaneity, creative involvement and meditation.

Humanity as such will reach it collectively in a later stage, through the intensification of the global consciousness. Something is bound to happen in that stage in the sense of a transformation and discontinuity. This has happened before in the evolutionary journey. This change is also a physical necessity if one considers the astronomical growth of the world's population. There may be different and new manifestations of the human.

Instinctively, human beings do not accept that the road to this new level of unified consciousness would be blocked through destruction of our planet.

It would seem that the human race feels and believes that its relationship with a higher order makes it a party to the commitment to complete the world. For what use? I think the more we become aware of the implicate and interrelated order and intentionality of the universe, our planet and humanity, the less we become interested in this question. The question originates from the limited scope of the world we live in and our reduced capacity, during the last two thousand years, to see beyond a homocentric worldview.

## Redefining Our Role

We must take into account a number of factors, if our function is to play an active and creative role in the completion of the evolution of the planet in the context of cosmogenesis. These factors are related to the notion of harmony. Not harmony in a static sense with a fixed balance of power, but in the sense of a moving, alternating interplay of a great number of factors, forces and fields, not necessarily in equilibrium, even sometimes far from equilibrium. A dynamic system within the context of a pattern, a "philharmonic" whole. A harmony that leads to progress as opposed to an equilibrium that leads to stagnation.

### INDIVIDUAL HARMONY

Confusion has resulted from increasing human consciousness, individual critical reflection, and the resulting elements of doubt and dualism. These elements of consciousness have led to a degree of disintegration and material orientation. Human beings form the building blocks of humanity and the noosphere. The reorientation of energy from disintegration to integration has to begin with the human individual. Harmony within the individual is essential for a constructive and positive completion of the world.

Those who have inner harmony, who follow a natural way and a pattern of creative functioning, achieve an inner balance of complementary and alternating forces. Such realized individuals contribute to evolution by their very functioning and by radiating energy to others.

Those who are not in harmony will analyze their individual and cultural codes and understand the underlying history of their lack of harmony. They will compensate negative forces they find with positive ones they develop. Such a balancing process leads to creative renewal of the individual.

Individual harmony is a necessity for constructive evolution. By definition, such individual harmony is possible because we originate from unity and the pattern of oneness is immanent within us. Understanding the origins of harmony and disharmony is essential for human individual development.

The restoration of original individual harmony is a major task in today's world. If this is not achieved by a substantial part of the world population, the course of evolution will be hazardous.

## SOCIAL HARMONY

Individuals are not isolated organisms with self-sufficient mental and physical capabilities. Interdependence and interrelatedness stem from our origins, and are recognizable throughout the universe. The latest findings in new physics confirm this. There is an implicate order of the cosmos of which all manifestations, including individual human beings, are part. Dynamic harmony, realized through complementary opposite forces, is the desirable state of human social systems and organizations: families, villages, states, international organizations, small enterprises, corporations, nonprofit organizations, unions, etcetera.

Historical evaluation of the origin, rise and background of disharmony allows for conscious reorganization. All of us have the opportunity to reorganize and revitalize a system, relation, organization or ourselves on the road to harmony by realigning the building blocks into a new order. This action contains the seeds of innovation. In this way, the dynamic disequilibrium in complex systems, parallel to recent discoveries in evolutive physicochemical systems, can form fertile ground for radical, unexpected and unpredictable "leaps" to higher levels of interrelation. This can be achieved through spontaneous and strong, localized fluctuations in the system.

GLOBAL HARMONY

The more harmonious individuals become, the more harmonious will be our social groupings, and the better our chance for global harmony. The individual or institutional contribution to global harmony is made increasingly easy and stimulating with the possibility of fast and effective global communication. There is an increasing reservoir of accessible data concerning social, political, scientific, philosophical and artistic facts, experiences and information. The global exchange of ideas by individuals and institutions provides substantial means for improving global harmony.

The first level of harmonious integration is individual. The second involves social organizations. The third level of global harmony is just evolving. Technologically there is no limit, yet global cooperation is under-developed. At this third level, the reconciliation of seemingly contradictory forces is extremely difficult to realize. The underlying disharmonies of individuals and organizations seem multiplied. Our present social organizations lack the ability to understand and act on the macroeffect of independent and uncoordinated micro-decisions. These micro-decisions occur within institutions, nations, corporations or political parties, and yet affect our global life.

The exponential growth of apparent global interdependence requires integration of micro and macro decision-making processes. This integration would be in sharp contrast to current trends in decision making, both democratic and autocratic. Both approaches use short-term survival codes for compartmentalized problem solving.

As individuals, we can contribute to a breakthrough to global dynamic harmony, by being creative within the social organizations in which we participate, and by looking for opportunities outside the present systems. The alternative to not finding solutions on this third level of global harmony is destruction of our planet, either through a one-time event such as a nuclear war or, more gradually, through extinction of the natural world via human plundering of resources and species.

Small groups of individuals must develop systems and technologies that can control and maintain harmony with nature at regional levels, thereby reducing the multiplicative effect of unbalanced regional handling of such basics as food, energy and waste.

The three levels of evolutionary environment—individual, institutional and global—offer many opportunities for the individual human being to fulfill a role in the realization of world harmony. Every individual plays a vital role, wherever he or she functions in this process and regardless of the scope of his or her social responsibilities.

The ability of small groups to change a system is supported by Prigogine's experimental results in physico-chemical systems. Similar transformations are identifiable in human social systems. The highly complex and imbalanced dissipative state of present human society, consuming vast amounts of energy and matter, would need only a limited number of active and interactive local fluctuation centers to cause a major transformation. Rupert Sheldrake adds that once new combinations or configurations have formed in groups of systems, this new know-how influences similar systems simultaneously through universal fields. These so-called morphogenetic fields are reformed by the new knowledge that is created. If these theories are correct and applicable universally to all kinds of systems, including human social systems, then these principles and fields could be the key factors in affecting the leap that seems immanent in the present phase of evolution on and around our earth.

# Present Trends in
# the World

The transition from the philosophically and personally oriented contents of the previous chapters to the down-to-earth aspects of the present situation in the world is quite abrupt. However, it is exactly this connection which is lacking and necessary to solve the global problems facing human society today. This chapter contains a change in emphasis, turning to facts and figures, graphs and tables, institutional reports and opinions, business and politics. The object is to show the interconnectedness of philosophies of life and evolution with the facts and figures emerging from an analysis of the "state of the world," (a phrase used by the World-watch Institute for their annual publication).

## Global Reports

Increasingly, with the great improvement in availability of information, assessments are made of the state of the world with regard to a variety of subjects, such as world population, natural resources, agriculture, industry and environment. There is a wealth of information in these reports, but the contents are too broad and too technical to reach the general public. Consequently, they are prepared and read mainly by specialists. It becomes increasingly important that the trends in our world be made known to a larger public in order to create a general awareness.

One of the first global reports to make an impact on public opinion was the Club of Rome's *The Limits to Growth* in 1972.[1] It created a general shock effect for the average citizen, who feared that within no time the world would run out of vital resources. A sense of crisis pervaded the atmosphere at the time of publication. The effect of this publication was counterproductive. The general public did not get or follow further information and the Club of Rome report receded into the background during the first oil crisis in 1973. Additionally, many people began asking themselves "Where are the catastrophes we were supposed to experience?" To be sure, there is great concern about poverty, inflation, unemployment, deficits and military spending, but this concern is not new. For many people, the effect of the first Club of Rome report was that there was a lot of noise about nothing.

The major difference between traditional concerns in our world and the Club of Rome report was that the former relate to cyclical, short-term and physically noticeable effects while the latter relates to directional, long-term and not yet physically noticeable effects. The Club of Rome report contains models of alternative scenarios; it is not a prediction of the future, as some people mistakenly suppose. People tend to get less excited about such long-term global evaluations, as they do not see or feel the implications.

In the early 1980s, five new global reports appeared:

*North-South: A Program for Survival*, report by the Willy Brandt commission, published in 1980

*The Global 2000 Report to the President: Entering The 21st Century*, report commissioned by Jimmy Carter (and disregarded by Ronald Reagan, as the subtitle of the pocket edition says), published in 1981

*World Development Report, 1980*, report by the World Bank in Washington, DC, published in 1981

*World Conservation Strategy: Living Resource Conservation for Development*, joint report involving major United Nations Agencies, published in 1980

*Interfutures: Facing the Future, Mastering the Probable and Managing the Unpredictable*, a report issued in 1980 by the Organization for Economic Cooperation and Development

Although these reports look at the global scene from different points of reference, there is a clear convergence of consensus about possible developments. There is an element of Teilhard's noosphere concept in the convergent views of these reports. The complexity and the size of these reports make it impossible to review their major conclusions completely. A very instructive summary and comparison of the five reports is available in a study by Magda Cordell McHale, *Ominous Trends and Valid Hopes*.[2]

The following major issues give an impression of the kind of observations dealt with in the reports mentioned:

- Every destiny-relevant trend, including population growth, seeming resource scarcities, and apparent threats to the global environment, turns out to be a gap in governance, a matter of management, an expression of human failure— that is, not a consequence of the "natural" order of things, not an expression of inherent limitations of a rich and versatile biosphere, but merely evidence that humankind is not yet managing the technosphere.
- In the short run—the next two or three decades—the human environment will deteriorate in all sorts of more or less predictable ways. The policy question is whether things will get worse before they get even worse, or will get worse before they get better. And that depends less on nature, (I repeat), than on us.
- We can no longer classify all problems as either "domestic" or "foreign," for many are both at the same time.
- Almost all governmental institutions have been designed, mandated and organized in keeping with academic disciplines, specialized professions, economic sections or technical functions—equipped, that is, to work on one problem at a time; the need today is not to isolate, but to integrate concepts, policies and programs of actions.
- On the basis of 1980 revisions and past facts, the world population, if there is no change in trend, shows the following pattern:

| year 1900 | 1,600,000,000 |
|-----------|---------------|
| 1950 | 2,500,000,000 |
| 1979 | 4,320,000,000 |
| 2000 | 6,160,000,000 |
| 2100 | 30,000,000,000 |

In the estimate for 2000, the Western world's population, including Russia's, will remain fairly constant and the growth will be in Africa and Asia; one third of the world's population will be Chinese.

- Global resources appear adequate for continued growth through the year 2000, but the distribution may prove to be inadequate.
- Fuelwood requirements for developing countries, where the bulk of the world population increase will occur, lead to a substantial and growing net nonrenewable loss of the world's forest resources.
- Mineral resources will continue to exist in adequate supply well past the turn of the century, but distribution and environmental impacts will restrict their effective use. Some minerals will probably be depleted completely between 2000 and 2050.
- Constant monitoring and assessment will be necessary in order to prevent the harmful effects of some technologies upon human health, natural systems and social stability.
- A new dimension of rapidly increasing interdependence of global financing has entered the world scene in the last thirty-five years and is reaching staggering proportions which are urgently in need of global management. All reports point to the importance of global governing of currency exchanges and interest costs which influence the cost of financing in such unpredictable ways.
- By the year 2000, human exploitation of the planet could result in a loss of up to 20 percent of the presently existing species, without any counterbalance or replacement. Nobody can predict what the impact of such a radical change in a matter of decades, will have on the total ecological system of the planet that took 4.6 billion years to evolve.
- The preservation of genetic diversity is both a matter of insurance and investment. The present food supply for humanity comes mainly from less than half a dozen species of crops and animals. Forty percent of the prescriptions used each year in the United States of America contain a drug of natural origin. Higher plants and animals are important therapeutic constituents, starting materials or models for synthesis.
- Biology knowledge will be increasingly applied to the majority of human activities, especially industrial activities. Some are already saying that biology will have as great an impact on industry in the twenty-first century as chemistry and physics did in the twentieth century.

- Some reports indicate the need for a new international economic order or reforms of the world economy, without indicating what this means and how this could be accomplished.
- Many recommendations are given for decentralized community involvement and regional management of food, energy and environment. These are bioregional models or areas.
- Increased attention should be paid to educating the public and the younger generation about the importance of international cooperation.
- The various government agencies, including the Environmental Protection Agency in the United States, are not able to integrate long-term planning and prevention of disharmonies and disasters because of the separation of many different disciplines. Currently, these agencies perform partial and corrective actions on processes already irreversible. These corrections are technically complex, time-consuming, bureaucratic, politically sensitive and subject to complicated legislation.
- Power and heat generation through nuclear fission is greatly delayed and is no longer the important contribution it was expected to be for the rest of the century. Nuclear fusion, solar, wind and other renewable energies will become important, clean sources in the twenty-first century. In the meantime, conventional energy generation from oil, gas, coal and wood will dominate for the coming decades, causing serious environmental pollution.

These observations from the reports clearly indicate the growing size and complexity of human society and our relatedness to nature and the limited resources of the earth. Most important is the stupendous acceleration in the various developments, the rapidly increasing size of the problems and the simultaneity of their occurrences.

The reports show the need for individual, social and global restoration of harmony, as discussed in the previous chapter, as well as the urgency of making the public aware of the situation. Political, corporate and governmental institutions are slow in their initiative and action because of their partly outdated structure and the limitations of their respective political and economical straight jackets. Public awareness, global consciousness of the massive process that is going on, and individual actions at the community level must be promoted to transform the present trend into constructive and coordinated management of our planet.

A new initiative became operational in the beginning of 1984, through the first publication of annual editions of *State of the World: A Worldwatch Institute Report on Progress Toward a Sustainable Society*, by Lester R. Brown.[3] These reports deal with selected major issues of the type covered in the five global reports mentioned above, but they have the great advantage of being published annually. As an example, the 1984 report presents a detailed analysis of the net loss of crop topsoil that is occurring in the world through mismanagement in soil preservation for agricultural use. At present, this amounts to a loss of 23 billion tons a year. This means a nonrenewable depletion of 7 percent per decade of the world's topsoil which produces food, feed and fiber. And yet, between 1955 and 1983, grain production in the world doubled, and will double again before 2000.

Another report on the global situation, *The Resourceful Earth*, by Julian L. Simon and Herman Kahn, was published in 1984.[4] The authors conclude that on all major issues of concern in previous global studies there is no reason for pessimism. On the contrary, they say sufficient counterforces are developing through market mechanisms and technological advances to turn situations around. These changes are occurring already. The study, however, lacks any evolutionary awareness of a more sophisticated, unified scale in the longer term. The wish seems the father of the thought that things will turn out all right within the context of the present paradigm. Resistance to change of paradigms is always great and, in this case, it clearly comes from representatives of the conservative factions of governments and corporations.

The report needs careful and professional attention, because the public becomes confused by the contradictions of highly qualified people. It is necessary to continuously review and correct presented data and information if there are new convincing facts available. The annual *Worldwatch Institute Report* would seem an ideal forum to formulate and incorporate these adaptations.

The reader must be careful in absorbing the information and statistics contained in these analyses. For example, *The Resourceful Earth* and *Worldwatch Institute Report* both make use of about ten major sources of qualified information regarding soil erosion, yet they have only one source in common and from that source they draw diametrically opposite conclusions.

Global reports nevertheless will play an important role in the process of creating public awareness. The reports draw attention to the need for integration of data on resource usage, and to the need for cooperation of all levels of awareness: individual, institutional and global. A relatively recent and influential example is 'Our Common Future' published by the World Commission on Environment and Development in 1987, Oxford, New York, Oxford University Press.[5]

The philosophies of Taoism and Teilhard provide patterns of personal, interpersonal and cosmic awareness. Such global perspectives, when integrated with present realities, give hopeful models for conscious action in the present and future. Both Teilhard and Taoism strongly emphasized the process of transformation that is fundamental to the course of events in nature. Both emphasized the need for a dynamic balance between seemingly opposite features in the manifestations of nature, humanity and the universe, and both emphasized the role of individual harmony within the context of global and universal harmony. A thorough understanding of and mental identification with their philosophies of life, as well as an awareness of the process that has led to the present situation of Western civilization, will pave the way to a new, creative approach to overcoming the danger of destructive discontinuities in the evolution of our earth.

## Decision Making Today

Previous chapters described the growing paradox between the exponential growth of global interdependence and the fragmented process of decision making by the world's major institutions, limited by their short-term survival codes. Gary Coates recently described this phenomenon in "Planning and the Paradox of Conscious Purpose," an essay in his book *Resettling America*, presenting examples of the counter-productive effect of short-term goals on long-term survival.[6]

The issue today is the unprecedented rate of development of global issues, the growing order of magnitude of their effects and their simultaneous manifestation. This process is taking place within a time span of decades in comparison with the billions of years it has taken the world to reach its present state. To illustrate this point, a random sample of Exponential Developments are presented in Figures 6.6–6.9. The reader will note that these developments concur with Teilhard's evolutionary scheme as presented in Figure 2.2.

The various curves from different sources, provided by Francois Meyer, Willis Harman, Rustin Roy and others, all have the striking phenomenon in common that the rate of change is accelerating considerably in the present era, leading to critical points in the first half of the twenty-first century. They quantify Teilhard's vision of a new discontinuity, although he thought in a much longer time span. Some years ago, Francois Meyer and others made calculations on the basis of a mathematical formula with regard to population growth. The application of this formula leads to dates between 2030 and 2070 as being the critical point where a transformational leap seems inevitable,

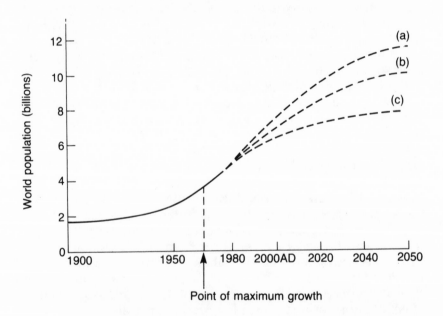

FIGURE 6.1 Predictions of future growth of world population by: (a) United Nations, (b) World Bank, (c) University of Chicago, showing slowing down of growth rate and eventual stabilization between 8 and 12 billion.

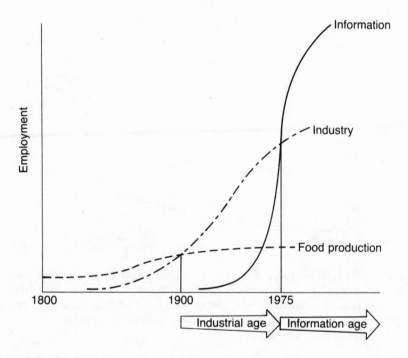

FIGURE 6.2 Changes in the number of people involved in different categories of human activity: food production, industry, and information processing.

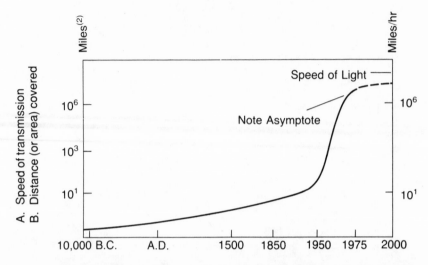

FIGURE 6.3   Weighted average of all information received. *Two points should be noted: first, in the developed world, most of our information transmission is at the absolute limit of the speed of light; second, the area of news gathering covers the whole world which contains everything that most humans are interested in.*

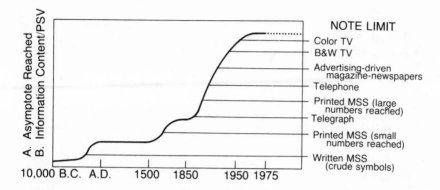

FIGURE 6.4  Qualitative data on the information revolution. *This graph makes the point that each innovation's impact eventually saturates at a new plateau. The latest plateau is qualitatively different since the receiver is now saturated.*

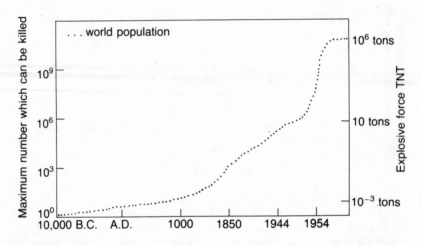

FIGURE 6.5 Destructive power. (Rustin Roy, *Experimenting with the Truth*)

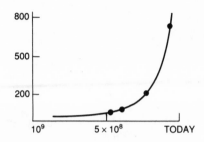

FIGURE 6.6 Increase in number of species in the oceans.
(François Meyer, *Teilhard et les Grandes Dérives du Monde Vivant*)

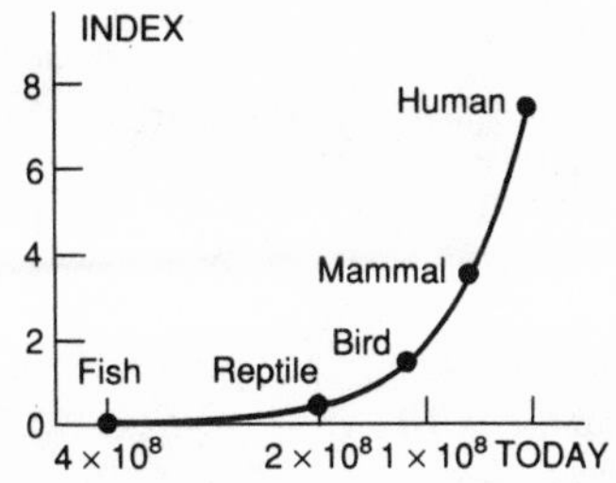

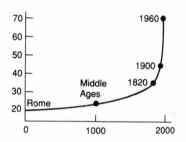

FIGURE 6.7 Development of the brains.
(François Meyer, *Teilhard et les Grandes Dérives du Monde Vivant*)

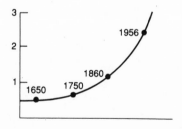

FIGURE 6.8 World population.
(François Meyer, *Teilhard et les Grandes Dérives du Monde Vivant*)

FIGURE 6.9 Average life expectancy.
(François Meyer, *Teilhard et les Grandes Dérives du Monde Vivant*)

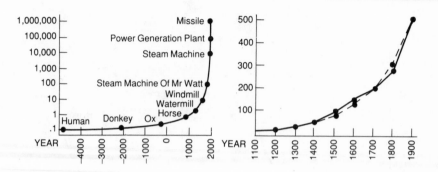

FIGURE 6.10 Inventions and discoveries.

FIGURE 6.11 Development of motoric power.

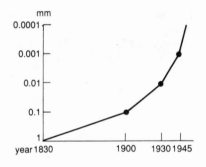

FIGURE 6.12 Degree of accuracy in engineering.

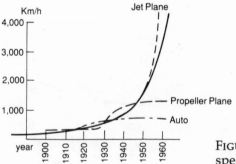

FIGURE 6.13 Development of speed.

(François Meyer, *Teilhard et les Grandes Dérives du Monde Vivant*)

A

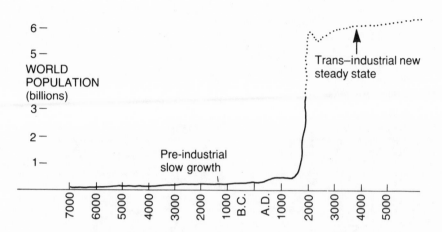

B

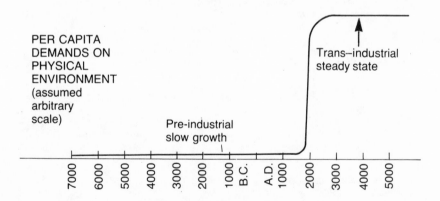

FIGURE 6.14 Two curves illustrating the uniqueness of the present point in history: (a) world population, and (b) per capita demands on the physical environment. (Willis Harman, *An Incomplete Guide to the Future*)

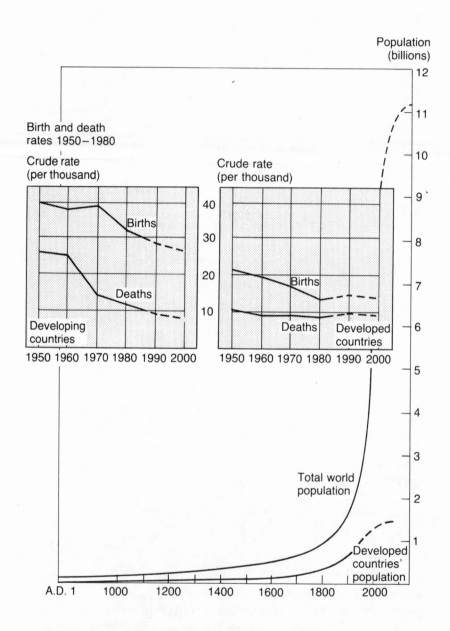

FIGURE 6.15   Past and projected world population.

whatever rational measures humankind develops in the field of birth control. A recent illustration of the situation is the graph presented in the *1984 World Development Report*[7] (see Figure 6.15).

The intriguing fact is that the exponential curve that describes the population development is of a type that apparently can be applied to many different manifestations occurring on our planet. Manifestations are of many different natures and they all seem to point in the same direction. As explained earlier in the context of evolution, the explosive nature of the exponential development would lead mathematically to an infinite level within a relatively short time. We know that such a limitless stage is impossible. In practice it means that a new level of orientation emerges and the trend is broken. The new level can be complete disintegration of the subject phenomenon or a different and new organization and coordination of its elements, leading to a new and different growth curve. Another possibility is a new mechanism in the phenomenon that leads to a stabilized position. The sample of curves shown indicates that at the turn of the twentieth century and in the first half of the next century, a great number of these discontinuities and transformations will become manifest. This observation, based on these and other indications, is supported by recent authors such as John P. Briggs and F. David Peat in *The Looking Glass Universe*,[8] Peter Russell in *The Global Brain*[9] and Willis Harman in *An Incomplete Guide to the Future*.[10] They all converge on the notion that fundamental changes will come about in a matter of decades.

An analysis of how decision-making bodies affect global developments and how counterproductive mechanisms work will lead us to answers about what we can do to control discontinuities, to affect transformations. Social systems and organizations must solve these problems and answer these questions. Of special importance in the transformation process are those groups that are out of touch with individual levels of awareness. These groups, such as nation states, larger corporations, major religious organizations, mass media, large educational institutions, trade unions and the legal profession, need to develop new levels of awareness to solve the global issues. The consensus within these institutions is that they know the risks and negative aspects of their decisions, but that they have either economically or politically no choice, because of short-term survival.

It is obvious that for long-term survival (and "long-term" is within one hundred years!) this attitude cannot be allowed to continue, apart from the fact that the institutions in many cases do not know the negative consequences. Examples, to name but a few, are the completely unforeseen effects on a regional and global scale of acid rain, $CO_2$ increase in the atmosphere, holes in the ozone layer, deforestation and chemical waste. There is not only the lack of knowledge, but also the additional factor of the vastly increasing impact at alarming speed of some of these interfering influences on the balance of nature.

Between institutions and the individual, there is a grey area of interconnecting organizations, communities and networks. This grey area is the most fertile soil that can be developed to transform attitude and action. The interface between individual, group and global consciousness is the focal point of change.

Large institutions are products of ideologies, theologies and economic theories that originate from circumstances very different from today's. Structures and categories have evolved, without fundamental adaptations, as if the surrounding context of evolution in the twentieth century did not exist. In most cases, ideologies are forgotten, theologies become obsolete and economic theories inconsequential. In general, institutional functioning in the world has become more and more based on reductionist, compartmental and linear attitudes.

The government of the United States has forgotten the transcendentalist spirit of the Founding Fathers; the Soviet government has forgotten the humanistic spirit of Marx; China is forgetting the Taoist and Confucian basis of their society; the Christian religion has moved away from its pure origin and yet does not accept the consequences of science and evolution; the multinationally operating corporations are differentiating ethical principles instead of integrating them; the mass media concentrate on irrelevant sensation instead of on relevant information; the large educational institutes are training specialists instead of universalists (as universities should). The structures of these institutions are, for the most part, traditional, hierarchical and financially capable of continuing their march through the changing world, like a supertanker through changing seas.

Adaptation to environment takes place in the context of the existing paradigm of technocratic excellence, profit optimalization and the market demand of the present human society.

This approach in the West has led to ever higher standards of living, with emphasis on financial, material and opportunistic political goals. A vast majority of populations in developed countries accept and enjoy this form of progress. The socialist movements in developed countries play the ambiguous role of participating in the wealth created by capitalist economies while ideologically opposing this system. They paradoxically want to protect the individual by depriving him or her of private initiative and responsibility. They confuse secular collectivity with divine oneness. In oneness, the individual flourishes in union. In collectivity, the individual perishes in fusion.

On the other hand, the Western system has moved too much into differentiation without union, leading to compartmental division in society.

The following table shows what this has led to:

| Institution | Main Market | Main Parameters | Main Philosophy | Main Financial Source |
|---|---|---|---|---|
| nation–state | voters citizens | law and order national product national defense national budget unemployment | ideology | taxes |
| corporation | customers | volume profit employment | continuity | cashflow shareholders banks |
| church | followers | | theology | contributions |
| media | public | volume profit employment | information | shareholders banks |
| education | pupils | status enrollment | knowledge | tuition grants |
| unions | members | membership labor contracts | employee protection | dues |

The problem confronting humanity and more specifically, the highly developed countries today, is that in the last five decades we have lived under the illusion that we could afford the paradox between short-term goals and long-term survival, and the separation of isolated decision-making within a total system because we have enough space and resources. Progress has

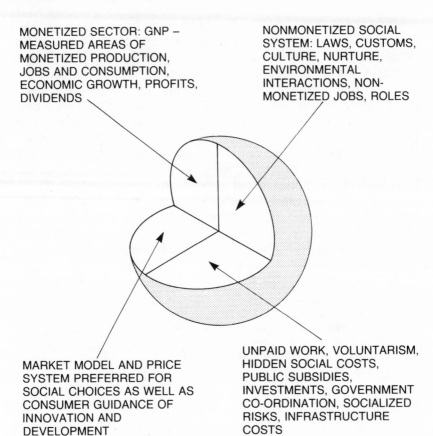

MONETIZED SECTOR: GNP – MEASURED AREAS OF MONETIZED PRODUCTION, JOBS AND CONSUMPTION, ECONOMIC GROWTH, PROFITS, DIVIDENDS

NONMONETIZED SOCIAL SYSTEM: LAWS, CUSTOMS, CULTURE, NURTURE, ENVIRONMENTAL INTERACTIONS, NON-MONETIZED JOBS, ROLES

MARKET MODEL AND PRICE SYSTEM PREFERRED FOR SOCIAL CHOICES AS WELL AS CONSUMER GUIDANCE OF INNOVATION AND DEVELOPMENT

UNPAID WORK, VOLUNTARISM, HIDDEN SOCIAL COSTS, PUBLIC SUBSIDIES, INVESTMENTS, GOVERNMENT CO-ORDINATION, SOCIALIZED RISKS, INFRASTRUCTURE COSTS

FIGURE 6.16   Schematic Diagram of Total Social Sphere (nonlinear, multidimensional, dynamic) hypothetically sectioned to show limited area mapped by economics.[11]

been measured solely on the basis of short-term homocentric parameters, but this progress does not mean progress for the whole earth anymore. And what is not good for the earth is also not good for humanity. The discrepancy now becomes acutely and increasingly untenable.

Managers of institutions must work with assumptions that have to be related to a broader context and not in isolation. However, we still lack the mentality, the organization and the experience to assess micro assumptions within a macro frame-work. National governments or international agencies will not be able to fulfill this role because a centralized system will kill decentralized initiatives and thereby the microfunctions of the system.

An important element in the solution of this dilemma is an efficient, reliable and continuously updated information system. At present we have all the necessary technology and media to have such a system. Unfortunately, we still use the technology and the media mainly to distribute wrong or incomplete information. In the present world of nation states and competitive business, this cannot be completely avoided for reasons of security and survival. A considerable improvement, however, is possible and necessary to upgrade our collective consciousness and unconsciousness.

Today many macroeconomic statistics and economic presentations do not reveal essential elements of the situation they are supposed to describe. Examples of this kind are the Gross National Product, the Dow Jones Average and the Annual Reports of corporations.

The GNP does not reflect activities that have no monetary reward or price. This refers to work in the household, do-it-yourself maintenance and barter-type transactions. Depending on the social and cultural structure of a specific society, these factors can cause a difference in the GNP of up to 20 percent. In addition, in some economies the so-called "black circuit" has reached a level of 10 percent or more of the GNP. Therefore, the GNP can be regarded less and less as a meaningful yardstick for the standard of living and the general economic condition of a nation. Moreover, neither important factors such as industrial waste, resource depletion and soaring replacement costs for public transportation systems—highways, subways, railways and airports—nor delayed maintenance costs are reflected in the GNP. Hazel Henderson describes and illustrates the fallacy of the GNP value in her book, *The Politics of the Solar Age*.[12] It is also emphasized by Lester Brown.[13]

The Dow Jones Averages of Industrials is regarded internationally as a valuable indicator for the performance and appreciations of the state of business in the United States. However, the Average contains only a limited number of listed companies. Apart from the fact that these companies represent a minimal percentage of the total share value of the New York Stock Exchange, the companies not listed are an even larger unrepresented group. These unrepresented companies are mostly the smaller ones—and the small ones do play a significant role in the development of employment, innovations and return on investment. In other words, the microworld of business is not reflected in the macroworld of statistics.

The Annual Reports of corporations have a strong "Newtonian" character. They use linear mathematical formulae to present and analyze their actions and transactions; everything is reduced finally to a figure, the so-called "bottom line." No insight can be obtained from these reports on the interdependence of the corporation within a broader system—national, international or global. No evaluation of the informal organization can be made from the report. Still we know, as recently emphasized in *In Search of Excellence* by Thomas J. Peters and Robert H. Waterman,[14] and *Managing* by Harold Geneen and Alvin Moscow,[15] how vital that aspect is for the success of a company. The result is that within a company different and essential information is available in addition to the facts and figures, but only these latter reach the public.

This brings us back to the general statement of the need for improvement of the completeness and the quality of information. Responsible decisions by good people, but within limited parameters and based on incomplete information, can lead to unacceptable situations in the longer term. Obviously, this has been the case throughout the history of the world. Today, however, the consequences in political, economical and ecological respects are more widespread, more intensively experienced and more influential to the survival of the earth than ever before. We have entered a period when change occurs at an ever-increasing speed and the consequences of policy decisions impact us in ever-larger orders of magnitude. Misjudgments will become exceedingly costly and cause irreversible damage. Therefore, all existing important indicators and yardsticks should be reviewed thoroughly and continuously checked for relevance. The main objective must be to bridge the gap that exists today between short-term and long-term values, between micro- and macroaspects of the same whole, not through rigid hierarchical bureaucratic models, but through information systems that reach and educate the decentralized parts of a natural society.

So long as the decentralized parts of society do not know and understand their relationship to the whole, the manager will only concentrate on making a profit, the politician on getting votes, the minister on spreading the gospel, the professor on teaching physics, the lawyer on winning litigations, the publisher on attracting readers, the union leader on negotiating contracts. If these responsible people were to investigate and understand, during a seminar, the magnitude of the problem we are heading for on this planet in the next, say, twenty to fifty years, they would still return to their jobs and continue as usual. This, by the way, is what happened to seminars on the issues of Club of Rome. We need a more consistent and continuous method of focusing the attention of decision makers to the global issues.

In the larger organizations of human cooperation, the emphasis is increasingly on the specific function of the individual within the total system. This function of the individual becomes more and more isolated from his or her individual personality as well as from the coordination center of the system with respect to relevant information and feedback. The effectiveness with which any human organization deals with this problem determines its organizational, political and financial survival.

Regardless of how well or even brilliantly organizations perform their role, the size and complexity, within the contexts of evolutionary patterns, eventually will lead to points of saturation and incapability of further coordination without fundamental change. Creative growth requires a leap to a new and different configuration and orientation. An interesting example is the split up of AT&T in the United States. The reasoning for this profound change in a large corporation is described in detail in Alvin Toffler's *The Adaptive Corporation*.[16]

Signs of saturation are increasingly observable tensions resulting from conflicts between the role of the individual employee in human organizations and his or her individual personality. Again, a gap between the macro- and microworld. On one hand, he or she has to maintain status and function within a system or organization that has developed into an alienating body with no natural and human relationships other than political, financial or mechanical. On the other hand, there is a personal and inner awareness of the problematic or unknown direction the system is following in the long run. Nothing can be changed in the short term if the system is running effectively and successfully from the perspective of its limited number of survival parameters.

Paradoxically, business corporations, as a group—including the best-run companies with the most successful and talented management—are delaying long-term progress toward a sustainable society. In a review of seventeen "policy statements" of large companies in Europe and United States, none has clear, sophisticated viewpoints of what impact their activities have on society in the long run. Growing disharmony in the world with regard to unbalanced social, ecological and financial irreversible processes will continue if the present structure of technological and economical goals is maintained.

Regrettably, the trend of the sixties and early seventies to present a social annual report in addition to a financial annual report, is reversing. The social reports, especially in the United States, are disappearing. Many companies have given up, because public interest is limited and things are going "so well" again that concentration is focused fully on financial, technical, commercial and national political issues.

The major question is how can the structure be revised and transformed, in time, to become in tune with radically new situations as they confront us over the next twenty to fifty years?

Within the time span that we have left, the "supertankers" that are the large institutions cannot be expected to adjust their course fast enough to avoid crashes.

An example of such an impending crash, in the short term, is the 1.4 trillion-dollar debt of the less-developed countries. This out-of-control situation is without rational solution and is maintained artificially against all rules of logic. Yet, the problem of increasing debt still may be solved with a lot of pain and political conflict because everybody "sees" the problem. This problem is, however, the tip of the iceberg. There exist numerous problems of the same magnitude, concerning energy, soil, unemployment, forest and species destruction, pollution, starvation and population explosion. The problem in the present phase of human society is that we only start to act— and even then most actions are inadequate and illusionary— when a development is reaching levels of near irreversibility.

Many of the major institutions mentioned historically have played an enormously important role in the achievements of Western civilization. Their contributions have included providing a decent standard of living for a large majority of the population, freedom from oppression and slavery, democratic government and freedom of speech, medical care, freedom of travel and worldwide communication. The next twenty to fifty years will require a new attitude, however, a new set of parameters and a radical change of course. It seems unlikely that the rigidity toward change and the self-satisfaction of the present compartmentally structured Western society will allow speedy transformation of their pyramid decision-making system. This system is largely unaware that it is nearing the end of its life cycle, an expression used in marketing strategies as well as in ecological analysis.

How can the change be achieved? The three possibilities are: confrontation, transformation and marginal action. Confrontation involves mass protests and legal procedures. Transformation involves changes within the systems and eventually of the systems themselves. Marginal action involves creating awareness and experiments on a limited scale inside and outside the systems on new frames of reference deviating radically from existing paradigms.

Today we see examples of all three alternatives. Confrontations are unavoidable if obviously destructive processes continue. Transformation is more desirable and philosophically more in parallel to the principles of Taoist and Teilhardian thought. However, the process will be mostly slow.

The marginal action route requires the vision and courage of individuals or small groups. Their actions will be localized fluctuations in society and will have the potential of creating radical changes in a broader scope. A parallel with Prigogine's concept of change comes to the mind.

Marginal action as an agent of change could be eventually the most important and effective one to result in a fundamentally different society.

## New Visions

Against the background of growing awareness of the inadequacy and future obsolescence of the systems described, there are many individuals, groupings and "networks" emerging in Europe and the United States that form signs of action for change. In the West, historically, the main pressure for change has come from socialist politics, primarily inspired by a desire for more equal distribution of wealth and power. The new movements for social change are primarily inspired by the need to prevent the destruction of our planet.

This development suggests that we are now entering the era of the ecological revolution. Ecological revolution will shift the center of attention from human progress to evolutionary progress of the whole planet. The whole life system of the biosphere will be looked at in further innovative and technologically corrective developments in the noosphere.

New movements are still largely informal and unstructured. They support a new approach that will lead to a higher level of human consciousness with harmonizing spiritual and material perspectives.

Previous chapters have indicated that this transformation of consciousness is a necessity and is predictable in the context of Teilhard's vision of the evolutionary development of the universe, our planet and humanity.

This combination of the necessity and the expectation of a transformation forms the foundation of new thinking. The new thinking is not a homogeneous, coordinated strategy, but rather a multidisciplinary voicing of a message that stems from a common awareness and a holistic approach toward the future. The simultaneous occurrence of all these different, emerging notions seems to be a manifestation of Jung's synchronicity principle and Teilhard's condensing noosphere. Marilyn Ferguson calls this new consciousness the "Aquarian Conspiracy."[17] Many leading authors frequently refer to Teilhard de Chardin and to Taoism as spiritual mentors.

The new visions come from scientists, philosophers, psychologists, environmentalists, futurists and feminists. Less active are businessmen, economists and theologians. Union leaders, educators, politicians and the media contribute little. Paradoxically, these last groups could have profound impact in new thinking because of their influence on the consciousness of so many people.

What are some of the active disciplines telling us?

**Scientists**, such as Fritjof Capra, Brian Swimme, Ilya Prigogine, Rustin Roy, Rupert Sheldrake, David Bohm, Erich Jantsch and P. C. W. Davies, are revealing the latest findings in new physics. The main items are as follows:

1. The cause-effect link for individual events has been found to be nonexistent at subatomic level (quantum physics).
2. There is a seamless web of information on relations throughout the universe and present everywhere (unified fields).

3. Relations create new identities and in this cosmogenic process the new codes are accessible throughout the universe (morphogenetic fields).
4. Most natural systems are not in equilibrium. A sufficient number of new relations in systems that are far from equilibrium can cause, after a short chaotic phase, a radically new system of a higher order of organization (self-organizing principle or thermodynamics of nonequilibrium systems).
5. All systems and relations contain dynamic interacting opposites.

The scientists come to the conclusion that these and other findings confirm religious, mystical and evolutionary visions of the oneness of the universe, the interconnectedness of everything tangible and intangible, and the assumption of one source, one way or divine will as found throughout all human stages of mythological, religious and intuitive thinking. After thousands of years, we are returning to the *philosophia perennis*.

The important consequence of this development is that the walls between the compartments of science, religion and philosophy now can be removed. This should contribute to a holistic approach to the future, especially if the younger generations become aware of the new findings.

**Psychologists**, such as Jean Houston, Abraham Maslow, Roberto Assagioli and Jean Bolen, are emphasizing the following concepts:

1. The individual can be made aware of the predominant accent Western civilization has given to the functioning of the so-called left-brain, the analytic, reductionist and masculine part; awareness of bipolar functioning can restore balance (yin-yang).
2. The mind and the brain have much more capacity and power than we are aware of, and individuals can train themselves in understanding, foster its functioning and thereby becoming more aware, harmonious and in touch with the universe.
3. The human individual, with a collective and individual subconscious level, a pure and unique self level, and an externally oriented ego level, can achieve harmony through understanding and integration of these three levels, thereby gaining access to oneness of the earth, the human being and the universe.

These developments open the way to wholeness and interconnectedness, and enable us to break through the limitations of the genetic and cultural codes that make us prisoners of ourselves. The integration of different potentials of the self will create individual maturity and harmony that is a condition for social and global harmony, and necessary for the transformation into a new phase of evolution.

**Environmentalists**, such as Lester Brown, Nancy and John Todd, Thomas Berry and Gary J. Coates, are emphasizing the following urgent needs:

1. To concentrate on the formation of "bioregions" where, on a self-sustainable basis, food production, energy generation and waste treatment are handled in a closed circuit, with community involvement, restoring balance between the organism and the environment. Several of these symbiotic communities are being developed successfully in various parts of the United States.
2. To investigate and publicize the ecological imbalances that are being created on a microscale and are affecting larger regions on a macroscale.
3. To change the accounting systems and improve accountability of companies and regions (provinces, states and nations, etcetera); to become aware of corporate effects on the stock of natural resources and their usage; to keep track of the resource balance sheet. Norway has developed innovative methods in this field.
4. To evaluate and identify which large-scale operations in the Western societies are likely to be of benefit in the future and which ones contain long-range, counter-productive potential.
5. To develop a strategy of long-term alternatives for large logistics systems such as highways, railways, airports and subways. Even if modernized, the present structure and systems will become practically irreplaceable physically, financially and ecologically. A society in transformation will have new values and initiatives to cope with this challenge.
6. To recognize that ecological considerations lead to sound economical and profitable investments, in the short- and long-term.

**Futurists**, such as Marilyn Ferguson, Barbara Marx Hubbard, Hazel Henderson, Willis Harman, John Naisbitt and Peter Russell are exposing us to the following facts:

1. Major trends in scientific, economic, social and individual development show signs of discontinuity, crisis and the potential of a leap forward to a new level of orientation.
2. The evolutionary process of the universe frequently has gone through phases of saturation, crisis and transformation. What appeared to be a threat turned out to be a blessing.
3. Decentralization to the individual, communal and smaller enterprise level is the trend that is rapidly taking shape in the United States in contrast with previous trends of centralization and large-scale organization. On one hand, there is growing alienation from large-scale pyramidical structures, while on the other hand, computerized information systems pave the way for smaller scale, flat structures.
4. A growing number of charismatic people, societies, institutes and networks inspires new thinking at all levels of society and create awareness at the individual level. The leaders of our major institutions, according to the self-organizing principle, eventually will follow the trend.

These futurists come from different personal and professional backgrounds, and their viewpoints converge on the irreversible process that leads to transformation. Observations and extrapolations indicate a time span of twenty to fifty years for fundamental transformation to take place. As the world has major regions where social, political, economic and technological status differ considerably in the phase of development, the transformation process will differ substantially from region to region. The new visions provide a pattern of thought and action within which the Western civilizations can initiate a process with global perspectives.

# Options for Action

Considerable gaps between phases of development in major regions of the world prevent a global approach at this stage. Western developed countries and Japan must take the lead in the transformation process and other regions will follow—hopefully before reaching the degree of saturation (or supersaturation) of the West and Japan.

We have roughly twenty to fifty years available to accomplish this transformation process, assuming that the one-time event of a nuclear war does not intervene. This is not much time, taking into account the "supertanker" nature of the present structures and systems. Initiatives for change in traditional institutions are not likely to come from the top down. The road of transformation leads from the bottom up—transformation, rather than confrontation in the sense of destruction of present structures and attitudes, followed by rebuilding the future, initiated by marginal action.

A regional, participatory approach will involve the individual within decentralized social groupings to form coherent social, geographical and ecological units. The size of these groupings will vary and depend on bioregional factors. These groupings must begin forming themselves within present community, state and national guidelines. Gradually they will become influential, and eventually they will transform the existing structure.

So long as nation states exist, and this, presumably, will be for a long time, regional groupings will remain subject to central authorities. These central authorities will be required to manage large, indispensable economy-of-scale operations as well as national defense, monetary policy, foreign policy and the national budget. This would have to develop into a management-by-exception structure rather than management-by-definition. In the United States, the policy and practice of decentralization is gaining momentum in a number of sectors of public life. An initiative called the Ozark Area Community Congress (OACC) resulted in four congresses in the early eighties, working out strategies and implementation programs for the bioregional concept in the United States. These conferences were attended by national and international participants.[1]

The recent explosive growth of new small enterprises in the United States (600,000 per year in 1983 compared to 93,000 in 1950), is supporting the trend toward regional and decentralized groupings. John Naisbitt, in *Megatrends*, describes regionalism and decentralization as already strongly emerging in the United States.[2]

Citizens of bioregional groupings must cooperate with two other major factors: large cities, and national and international corporations. Citizens of the bioregions who are employed by these institutions may form groups as bioregion representatives and become effective and motivated agents of marginal activity. Such representative groups could become important promoters of transformation within and between the corporations and city management. Present institutions will remain intact and carry out their present responsibilities, but a new element of "bioregional consciousness" is introduced within and between organizations. The advantage of this approach is that there will be less bureaucracy, and the distance between the representatives and the region they represent will be smaller than that of existing democratic political structures and federal agencies.

In many ways, early democracies exemplify bioregionalism. The second-oldest democracy in the world, Switzerland (the first being Iceland), operates in this way. The type of leadership this system produces is evident in Switzerland, where the presidency rotates among the cabinet members.

Gradual transformation through individual involvement is a logical and creative translation of the visions of Taoism, Teilhard and new thinking. We are in the process of reaching a saturation point in our present Western society. The signals of change are present in the condensing noosphere. Dissatisfaction is growing. If the self-organizing principle of Prigogine can be applied to human populations, only a small percentage of new and creative thinking is necessary to bring about a new global orientation.

A period of chaos may precede such creativity, as indicated by Jay Forrester in his system dynamics model of the national economy of the United States.[3] Although the United States is presently showing an economic downturn, this downturn is part of a short business cycle. The long-wave cycle (forty to sixty years) shows that an economic collapse similar to that which occurred in 1930 may occur before the end of the century. The period of chaos and disorientation that will follow may lead to the natural disappearance of a number of traditional power centers in the present economic structure. Large, heavy-industry giants may not survive. The new creative centers in the smaller, high-technology sector and the bioregional activities will have the best opportunity for further development. A new order will arise out of chaos.

The transformation process requires many, informal, natural leaders who can communicate with sophistication, inspiration and common sense the message of the new paradigm. The new paradigm is constructive and not destructive. It should be based on a discontinuity within an evolutionary process, where existing building blocks are to be integrated in new configurations. Most of the building blocks we have today are valuable elements of the work of past generations.

Confrontational approaches, if not meant to destroy, sometimes can be unavoidable to make the issue clear, and to force unreasonable resistance; but if driven too far, they will be counterproductive. The present rapid growth and quality of societies, institutes, networks and literature aimed at public awareness of alternative futures are important instruments for the implementation of a constructive transformation.

Information is a major element in the process of transformation, as is emphasized in John Diebold's *Making the Future Work*[4] and Peter Russell's *The Awakening Earth*.[5] Western society has become very effective in the field of communications, but there is the need for a considerable shift in the ''software,'' meaning the programs used. Educational institutions, religious institutions and the media can and should make a major effort to adapt the software and produce relevant information about the evolutionary state of the world. The world will change when individuals, and especially the new generations, have profound information on the process that has led humanity from tribal to modern society, from the agricultural to the industrial revolution, from a respect for nature to a throw-away mentality and a wonderland orientation.

Education in schools and universities, parallel to

specialization, should develop a standard program of information on how humanity arrived where we are today and how we have entered the era of the ecological revolution, shifting the emphasis on progress from humanity to the total life system. These perspectives are not represented today in any university programs in Europe or the United States.

Global transformation necessitates that religious institutions take an active position in the reconciliation of modern science and basic religious thinking, thereby contributing to the understanding of unity and harmony in the universe and of humanity's relation to a higher order of existence. Religious institutions must globalize their values to help restore the balance between humanity and nature, a subject they neglect today. The present emergence of true interreligious dialogues on a global scale and the common search for unifying and complementary aspects of the world religions is an encouraging step in the right direction.

The enormous potential of the media to contribute to the information on the past, present and future of our planet should be utilized to the full. The media should devote a good part of their technological and journalistic capabilities to public education to cover the story of our planet and the need and the chance for survival. Public awareness of the planetary dimension of the ecological revolution of the twenty-first century must have a profound and lasting influence on the preservation of peace and nature on the planet.

The preservation of nature has to be the common goal of all of humanity, whether North American, Russian, European, Japanese, South American, African or Asian, and is becoming a major issue of the United Nations. For this vital purpose, there is the need and the challenge for the United Nations Organization to add philosophical and religious dimensions to its agenda, which at present is mainly political. It is not surprising that U Thant, Dag Hammerskjold, Javier Perez de Cuellar and Robert Muller were and are profoundly influenced by Teilhardian thought. The United Nations offers, in principle, a unique vehicle for convergence of human consciousness on a global scale. Unfortunately, political aspects dominate the scene and jeopardize progress on the short term. It may be that a common goal of all nations—the preservation of the nature of earth—can provide a new dimension of cooperation that surpasses political and ideological barriers. A challenge the United Nations organization can hardly ignore!

# Conclusion

Approximately 18 billion years ago, the universe somehow started to unfold. Out of the void, radiation manifested itself and subsequently energy and matter, leading to a succession of phenomena, from the smallest elementary particle or wave to the most complex organism: the human.

The unfolding process shows a pattern of growth through differentiation, union and complexity. At various intervals, radically new combinations emerge as existing systems reach saturation points: atoms, molecules, cells, organisms. Implicitly, these increasingly complex manifestations reveal other phenomena: life, sex, consciousness, self-reflexive consciousness.

Complex systems showing life characteristics so far have been observed and experienced only on earth, a planet that came into existence approximately 4.5 billion years ago.

Within the unfolding process of the universe, the earth developed a geosphere (inorganic matter), a biosphere (living organisms) and a noosphere, a Teilhardian term. The noosphere is a rapidly condensing layer of conscious and unconscious spiritual and mental thought, knowledge and understanding of humanity.

Life on earth originated approximately 3.5 billion years ago; the human, self-reflexive being emerged approximately 3 million years ago. This led to the beginning of the unfolding of the noosphere.

The unfolding of the noosphere, embracing expanding individual and collective human thought, inspirations and experience, led initially to the ancient religious and tribal worldviews. Until approximately two thousand five hundred years ago, the emphasis was on the collective spirit, nature, mythological deities, symbols and ever-returning cycles.

Between 800 B.C. and 200 B.C., the condensing noosphere reached a kind of saturation point. From Greece, through Palestine, Persia, India and China—independently and simultaneously—a new pattern of thought emerged: the consciousness of individual critical reflection. This transformation freed the human spirit from nature, allowed the individual to discover the image of God and to have an individual viewpoint in judgment of the state and religion. The individual could seek truth through dialectic processes.

The development of critical reflections shaped the great philosophies and the great religions. Most of the new thinking alienated humans from their rootedness in the geosphere and the biosphere, and led to a radical distinction between the physical world and the divine or ultimate reality. Taoism considered divine and earthly values as mutually inclusive in the oneness or unity of the universe, the earth and the human being. Taoism maintained unity within differentiation. Judaic and Confucian thought opened the way to secularization, Buddhism and Hinduism to spiritualization.

Judaism, the transformation of Jewish consciousness, became the base for the later emergence of Christianity as well as Islam. In addition to the mystical and divine dimensions of the concept of the Trinity (Father, Son and Holy Ghost), the Christian culture introduced historicity as a fundamental aspect of the human and universal story. Developmental time superimposed on cyclical time became a cornerstone of Western homocentric thought.

The road of radical distinctions was pursued further in Christian dogmatic developments in the West. Rational and intellectual dogmas categorized the mystic element in Christian thought. Greek philosophy and Roman legality entered the foundations of the Church, culminating in Thomas Aquinas' formulations of the Christian principles in the thirteenth century.

Distinctional and rational thinking, combined with the supposition of divinely guaranteed patterns governing the events in the world, led to the Western scientific approach of analyzing, reducing, synthesizing and measuring the material and natural world. The individual and collective search for Truth led to theoretical concepts, explaining and predicting mechanical relationships. The mechanistic mind entered and dominated the noosphere from the sixteenth century through the works of Galileo, Newton, Descartes and others.

In the nineteenth century, a new mechanism was discovered: natural selection in the development of biological species. Darwin's thesis, coinciding with Lyell's discovery that the earth was eons old, opened the way for evolutionary theories. These were opposed to the principle of the fixity of separately created species and the biblical story of the creation of the earth, which supposedly occurred in 4004 B.C.

Eastern and Far Eastern civilizations maintained their cultural codes of spirituality and cyclical time. Chinese thinking, influenced by nature-oriented Taoism and society-oriented Confucianism, developed technologies and alchemy, based on observations of natural processes and human experience. Scientific progress and synthesis based on concepts, analysis and reduction predominantly developed in the West.

The science-based technologies in the West developed ever-larger-scale operations during the nineteenth century, resulting in the industrial revolution. The industrial revolution promoted size, quantity, division of labor and new power structures next to the State and the Church.

This new organizational dimension in human society led eventually to an increase in the speed of the evolutionary process. Within a hundred years, the natural senses of the human being were and are extended in comparison with the billions of years of natural, genetic and planetary evolution. The microscope and telescope are examples of profound "leaps" that have expanded the range of the senses even though the physical human body has not evolved further. The noosphere is rapidly condensing with human inventions, knowledge and understanding that is universally available for collective and individual use without having to repeat the process of specialization. The noosphere is developing a strong collective dimension.

The process of human alienation from nature that was initiated two thousand five hundred years ago with conceptual and mechanistic developments was strengthened further by human domination over nature. Humankind's transformation of nature's vegetation, minerals and animal forms for human goals took place at an increasing rate, on an unlimited scale. In addition, an alienation of individuals within humanity began to emerge. The industrial structure disrupted social relationships. The craftsperson's identification with a total product was replaced by the specialist's limited interest in a part. Karl Marx protested against this situation by developing new concepts of social structures; they were based on a mechanistic and dialectic worldview, supported by contemporary Darwinistic evolutionary thinking.

In the beginning of the twentieth century, psychology and physics introduced a new phase in Western thought with the notions of relativity and wholeness. The importance of this leap in the noosphere is comparable to the transformation from collective to individual and reflective critical thinking two thousand five hundred years earlier. Einstein and Jung were exponents of this new line of relative and holistic thinking. This new phase marked the arrival of an era of Western thinking in the direction of interconnectedness, integration, wholeness and relations.

In the meantime, Western technological momentum was in full swing, leading to more inventions and new applications. The philosophical and humanitarian consequences of the new relativistic and holistic thinking were not yet apparent. The industrial revolution led to the atom bomb and an exponential growth of technology, welfare, social security, medical care and the general standard of living in the West after World War II.

In science, the trend toward integrative thinking was complemented by dynamic thinking. the developmental, goal-oriented and directional foundation of the Christian culture eventually contributed to orienting Western scientific thinking towards the notion of irreversible change. The holistic approach that was still mainly spacially oriented became integrated with the dynamic dimension of evolutionary thinking. A temporary negative aspect of the concept of irreversible change included the related concept of entropy, leading to doom thinking on the eventual death of the universe in ultimate chaos. Later and recent discoveries of self-organizing principles in nature (inorganic and organic) correct this notion.

In the midst of these profound changes in Western thinking, Teilhard de Chardin developed his integrative and dynamic vision on the evolution of the universe: cosmogenesis in a Christian context. According to his theory, the cosmos, the earth and humanity participate in a dynamic process with a pattern and an intentionality. During the process, growing complexity leads to increased consciousness. Teilhard affirmed the participation of the human being in both the earthly and the divine world. Humanity is at the spearhead of evolution which will reach its culmination at the omega point, when a new transformation of consciousness will emerge through the noosphere.

In the course of the twentieth century, scientific inventions and discoveries developed exponentially, partly as a result of intensified interactions between scientists and partly because more scientists emerged. The world population grew from 1.6 billion in 1900 to 5 billion in 1989. New laws and concepts did not invalidate old ones, but superseded them in a broader context.

Since the 1960s, a universal dimension has been added to the holistic and the dynamic aspects of science and psychology. The universe appears a seamless web. Patterns and codes that manifest themselves on earth are part of a universal, unfolding whole. The forces and agents of change operate within existing codes and patterns, but also create new ones. These forces consistently defy entropy and are of a self-organizing nature. Science discovers universal intentionality in all creative processes. Unique and unpredictable manifestations are recognized in contrast to statistical averages, which are products of the mind but not of ultimate reality. The views of Prigogine, Bohm and Jung converge here.

Teilhard, Taoism and the new physics share the notion of the all-pervading interconnectedness of the earth, human beings and the universe. Radical distinctions do not fit in this thinking. The original wisdom of Taoism provides a strengthening, complementary element to new awareness in Western thinking. The coincidence of spirit and matter, psychology and physics, individuality and wholeness, life and death, male and female, small and large, beginning and end as complementary opposites is present in both Taoism and new Western thinking. Taoism achieves harmony by following the universal pattern to its origin, Western thought by following it to its intention. Essentially, both find space- and timeless ultimate reality. Taoism and Western thinking form complementary opposites.

The global interconnectedness of local events and forces is becoming increasingly apparent in political, financial and industrial areas. These human activities are directed by institutions that operate within a survival context containing a limited number of parameters. These parameters are of a mechanistic nature, a model now surpassed in science, psychology and philosophy.

Global reports on major issues like financing, world populations, natural resources and ecology illustrate the increased interconnectedness. The main factors here are the rapid rise in the order of magnitude, the intensity and the simultaneity of all these major developments. It represents the kind of condensing process that is part of Teilhard's evolutionary vision. Application of system dynamics models of Jay Forrester, linking micro-and macrophenomena, will be important tools for understanding the process and what should be done about it.

In the evolutionary process, the human organism has formed families, communities, associations, corporations, institutions, networks, large corporations and nation states. In this range of combinations, the larger corporations and the nation states reach a size and complexity that seems to be near a saturation point. In parallel with previous similar saturation points in the planetary evolution process, as described by Teilhard, a transformation to a new consciousness, a new orientation and configuration will occur. Extrapolation of important developments in human society, such as world population, indicates that a transformational leap seems likely within one hundred years.

Actions to prepare and achieve a radically new situation require a new attitude of the individual and institutions toward their functioning and their influence on the state of the world. The new transformation of humanity will not be reached if the earth is destroyed instantly by nuclear war or gradually by artificial disruption and destruction of the biosphere. Both Teilhardian and Western thinking need to become more biocentric and less homocentric. Individual harmony, social harmony and eventually global harmony are the required environment for a transformation to occur. Progress for the whole earth system will supersede progress for human society, which will thereby survive.

Actions for change will be based on a new relationship between the individual and his or her surroundings. With regard to natural environment, the emphasis will be on bioregional models, integrating human needs and existing natural conditions and resources. With regard to organizational surroundings, individuals will participate in the bioregional communities. The emphasis will be on technical decentralization and high quality information, supported by the newest technology. Ecology will enter the decision–making process in larger corporations and nation states from the bottom up with priority on prevention; this in contrast to the from the top-down method with priority on control.

Large corporations and governments will regroup their activities into those where large-scale operations can remain meaningful in the long term and those where small-scale operations will be the survival model and functional within the ecological community. The last group will be developed in de-centralized communities and companies. In addition to social, political, economic and technological factors, the economics of ecology will play an increasingly important role in the decision-making process leading to restructuring. The restructuring transformation will be accomplished by internal and external confrontational and marginal actions.

Educational, religious and media institutions will adapt their attitude and apply their skills to supply relevant information to educate citizens and decision makers about the essentials of the evolutionary process we were and are part of. These institutions will show us how we can redefine our role to contribute con-structively to this process. This will lead to an acceptable level of fulfillment in life. Schools, universities, churches and media have a heavy responsibility in making this work. There is no lack of technological hardware, but better software is needed.

International institutions will play a major role in realizing the required attitudes at an international and global level and guid-ing Western societies from the industrial age to the ecological age. The defense of our earth transcends political and ideo-logical barriers, and will contribute significantly to the preservation of nature as well as to the preservation of peace.

In conclusion, everything should be done to ensure that humanity becomes intensely conscious of its vital position and role in the evolutionary process of the earth and the universe. Then and only then will the decision-making process in human society change. The change will be affected by new personal attitudes, new community attitudes and new government and corporate attitudes—attitudes that will reflect intellectual and emotional awareness of the principle of interconnectedness in nature, the recent stupendously accelerating manifestations of human activities, the evolutionary patterns and intentionality of a universal process and the uniqueness of individual events and beings.

The resulting transformation can be expected and is needed within the next fifty years if our planet is to survive.

# Notes

*CHAPTER ONE: Distinction and Unity*

1. Chang Chung-Yuan, *Tao: A New Way of Thinking. Tao Te Ching*, chapter 25, p. 71.

2. Karl Jaspers, *The Origin and Goal of History*, trans. Michael Bullock (New Haven: Yale University Press, 1953).

3. *Bonaventure and the Coincidence of Opposites: The Theology of Bonaventure*, ed. Ewert Cousins (Chicago: Franciscan Herald Press, 1978).

4. Chang Chung-Yuan.

5. Fox Butterfield, *China: Alive in the Bitter Sea* (New York: Times Books, 1982).

6. Pierre Teilhard de Chardin, *The Divine Milieu*, trans. Bernard Wall (London: William Collins Sons & Co., Ltd., and New York: Harper & Brothers, 1960), pp. 52-3.

7. Pierre Teilhard de Chardin, *Toward the Future*, trans. Rene Hague (London: William Collins Sons & Co., Ltd., and New York: Harcourt Brace Jovanovich, Inc., 1975), pp. 146-7.

8. Ibid., p. 140.

9. Henri L. Bergson, *Creative Evolution* (London: MacMillan & Co., Ltd., 1964).

10. Carl G. Jung, *The Undiscovered Self* (London: Routledge & Kegan Paul, 1958), p. 47.

11. Colin A. Ronan, *The Shorter Science and Civilisation in China*, vol. 1 (Cambridge: Cambridge University Press, 1978.)

12. Pierre Teilhard de Chardin, *Human Energy* (London: William Collins Sons & Co., Ltd. and New York: Harcourt Brace Jovanovich, Inc., 1969).

13. Pierre Teilhard de Chardin, *The Phenomenon of Man*, trans. Bernard Wall (London: William Collins Sons & Co., Ltd., and New York: Harper & Brothers, 1959), pp. 64–5.

14. Paul Hawken, *The Next Economy* (New York: Holt, Rinehart & Winston, Inc. 1983).

15. Thomas Kuhn, *The Structure of Scientific Revolutions* (Chicago: University of Chicago Press, 1970).

16. Chang Chung-Yuan, p. 52.

17. Pierre Teilhard de Chardin, *L'Apparition de l'Homme* (Paris: Editions du Seuil, 1956), p. 70.

18. Ilya Prigogine and Isabelle Stengers, *Order Out of Chaos: Man's New Dialogue with Nature* (New York: Bantam Books, 1984), pp. 12–13, 22.

19. Gary J. Coates, *Resettling America: Energy, Ecology, and Community* (Acton, MA: Brick House Publishing Co., 1981), p. 525.

20. Joseph Needham, *Science and Civilisation in China*, vol. 5, part 5 (Cambridge: Cambridge University Press, 1972), p. 293.

21. Bede Griffiths, *The Marriage of East and West* (London: William Collins Sons & Co., Ltd., 1982), p. 178.

22. Prigogine and Stengers, p. 15.

23. Rupert Sheldrake, *A New Science of Life: The Hypothesis of Formative Causation* (Los Angeles: Jeremy P. Tarcher, Inc., 1981).

24. Dennis Gabor, *Inventing the Future* (London: Secter and Warburg, 1963).

25. Prigogine and Stengers, pp. 12–13.

26. Erich Jantsch, *The Self-Organizing Universe: Scientific and Human Implications of the Emerging Paradigm of Evolution* (Oxford: Pergamon Press, 1980).

27. David Bohm, *Wholeness and the Implicate Order* (London: Ark Paperbacks, 1983).

28. Barbara Marx Hubbard, *Evolutionary Journey: A Personal Guide to a Positive Future* (San Francisco: Evolutionary Press, 1982), p. 145.

29. Wing-Tsit Chan, *A Source Book in Chinese Philosophy* (Princeton, NJ: Princeton University Press, 1973), p. 79.

30. *Tao Te Ching*, trans. Lin Yu Tang, p. 229.

31. Chang Chung-Yuan, p. 109.

32. Richard Wilhelm and C. G. Jung, *The Secret of the Golden Flower: A Chinese Book of Life* (New York: Harcourt Brace Jovanovich, 1962), p. 13.

33. Wing-Tsit Chan, pp. 588–634.

34. Teilhard de Chardin, *Le Milieu Divin*. (New York: Harper & Brothers, 1960).

35. Teilhard de Chardin, *The Phenomenon of Man*, p. 45.

36. Teilhard de Chardin, *The Heart of the Matter*, p. 20.

*CHAPTER TWO: Change*

1. Chang Chung-Yuan, p. 118.

2. Charles Darwin, *On the Origin of Species* (London: Ward Lock & Co., Ltd., 1910).

3. Charles Lyell, *Principles of Geology* (London: John J. Murray, 1834).

4. Prigogine and Stengers, pp. 12–13.

5. *The I Ching or Book of Changes*, trans. Richard Wilhelm (New York: Bollingen Foundation, Inc., and Princeton, NJ: Princeton University Press, 1950).

6. *Chuang Tzu*, trans. Herbert A. Giles, (London: Bernard Quaritch, Ltd., 1926), p. 220.

7. Yves Raguin, *Lecons sur le Taoisme* (Taipei: Publications de l'Association Française Pour Le Development Cultural et Scientifique en Asie, 1981), p. 71.

8. Teilhard de Chardin, *The Future of Man* (New York: Harper & Row, Publishers, Inc. 1964) p. 88.

9. *Gaudeum et Spes*, Second Vatican Oecumenic Council, session IX, December, 1965.

10. *Humani Generis*, Discours du Pape et Chronique Romaine, (lettre encyclique 12 Aout 1950), supplement au no 167 Janvier 1966.

11. *Les Memoires Historiques de Se-ma-Ts'ien* (Paris: Leroux, 1895–1905).

12. R. G. H. Sin, *Ch'i: A Neo-Taoist Approach to Life* (Cambridge MA: The MIT Press, 1974), p. 52.

13. Helmut Wilhelm, *Change* (Princeton: Princeton Press, 1960), p. 20.

14. C. G. Jung, *An Acausal Connecting Principle* (London: Routledge & Kegan Paul, 1955) pp. 49–52.

15. Joseph Needham, *The Grand Titration: Science and Society in East and West* (London: Allen & Unwin, 1969), p. 266.

16. St. Thomas Aquinas, *Compendium Theologia*, chapter 3.

17. C. Rau, *Philos. Rev. 62.*

18. Pierre Teilhard de Chardin, *Mon Univers* (Paris: Editions du Seuil, 1965), p. 119.

19. *Chuang Tzu: The Inner Chapters*, ed. A. C. Graham (London: Unwin Hyman, 1981), p. 29.

20. *Tao Te Ching*, chapter 51.

21. Teilhard de Chardin, *The Divine Milieu*, p. 114.

22. Marie-Ina Bergeron, *La Chine et Teilhard* (Paris: Editions Universitaries, Jean Pierre Delarge, 1976), pp. 38–41.

**CHAPTER THREE:** *Human Values*

1. Chang Chung-Yuan, p. 32

2. Graham, p. 183.

3. Chang Chung-Yuan, p. 47

4. Ibid., p. 95.

5. Ibid., p. 131

6. Graham, p. 183.

7. Claude Larre, *Le Traite VII du Huai Nan Tzu* (Paris: Institut Ricci, 1982), pp. 102–3.

8. Martin Heidegger, *On Time and Being* (New York: Harper & Row, Publishers, Inc., 1972).

9. Thome H. Fang, *The Chinese View of Life* (Taipei: Linking Publishing Co., Ltd., 1980), pp. 53–4.

10. Chang Chung-Yuan, p. 166.

11. Ibid., p. 166.

12. Chan, p. 177.

13. Teilhard de Chardin, *Le Milieu Divin*, p. 86.

14. Ibid., p. 149.

15. Bertrand Russell, *Marriage and Morals* (London: George Allan and Unwin, 1976).

16. *Tao Te Ching*, chapter 6, p. 173.

17. Ibid., chapter 28, p. 204.

18. Ibid., chapter 52, p. 235.

19. Sukie Colegrave, *The Spirit of the Valley* (London: Virago, 1979).

20. Teilhard de Chardin, *The Heart of the Matter*, p. 60.

21. Philip Rawson and Laszlo Legeza, *Tao: The Chinese Philosophy of Time and Change* (London: Thames and Hudson, 1973), pp. 7–32.

22. Confucius, *The Book of Rites* in Legge's *The Texts of Confucianism* (Oxford: 1899).

23. *Mo Tzu: Basic Writings*, trans. Burton Watson (New York: Columbia University Press, 1963), pp. 110–116.

24. Teilhard de Chardin, *Toward the Future*, p. 88.


*CHAPTER FIVE: Emerging Worldview*

1. William Theodore de Bary, *Sources of Chinese Tradition* Volume 1 (New York: Columbia University Press, 1960), p. 51.


*CHAPTER SIX: Present Trends in the World*

1. Dennis L. Meadows, *The Limits to Growth* (New York: Universe Books, 1972).

2. Magda Cordell McHale, *Ominous Trends and Valid Hopes: A Comparison of Five World Reports* (Minneapolis, MN: Hubert H. Humphrey Institute of Public Affairs, University of Minnesota, 1981).

3. Lester R. Brown, *State of the World, 1984: A Worldwatch Institute Report on Progress Toward a Sustainable Society* (New York: W. W. Norton & Co., 1984).

4. *The Resourceful Earth: A Response to Global 2000*, eds. Julian L. Simon and Herman Kahn (Oxford: Basil Blackwell Publishers, Ltd., 1984).

5. *Our Common Future* by the World Commission on Environment and Development (Oxford, New York: Oxford University Press, 1987).

6. Coates, p. 525.

7. *World Development Report 1984*, p. 3.

8. John P. Briggs and F. David Peat, *The Looking Glass Universe* (New York: Simon and Schuster, 1984), p. 14.

9. Peter Russell, *The Global Brain: Speculations on the Evolutionary Leap to Planet Consciousness* (Los Angeles: J. P. Tarcher, Inc., 1983), p. 199.

10. Willis W. Harman, *An Incomplete Guide to the Future* (New York: W. W. Norton & Co., Inc., 1979), p. 37.

11. Hazel Henderson, *The Politics of the Solar Age: Alternatives to Economics* (New York; Anchor Press (Doubleday, 1981), p. 29.

12. Hazel Henderson, *The Politics of the Solar Age: Alternatives to Economics* (New York: Anchor Press/Doubleday, 1981), p. 29.

13. Brown, pp. 196-7.

14. Thomas J. Peters and Robert H. Waterman, Jr., *In Search of Excellence: Letters from America's Best-Run Companies* (New York: Harper & Row, Publishers, Inc., 1982), pp. 42, 53, 109.

15. Harold Geneen and Alvin Moscow, *Managing* (New York: Doubleday & Co., Inc., 1984).

16. Alvin Toffler, *The Adaptive Corporation* (New York: McGraw-Hill Book Co., Inc., 1985).

17. Marilyn Ferguson, *The Aquarian Conspiracy: Personal and Social Transformation in the 1980s* (Los Angeles: J. P. Tarcher, Inc., 1981).

**CHAPTER SEVEN:** *Options for Action*

1. Charlene Spretnak and Fritjof Capra, *Green Politics: The Global Promise* (New York: E. P. Dutton, 1984), pp. 204-6.

2. John Naisbitt, *Megatrends* (New York: Warner Books, Inc., 1988).

3. Jay Forrester, "Information Sources for Modeling the National Economy," *Journal of the American Statistical Association*, vol. 75, no. 371, Sept. 1980, p. 25.

4. John Diebold, *Making the Future Work* (New York: Simon and Schuster, 1984), p. 417.

5. Peter Russell, *The Awakening Earth* (London: Routledge & Kegan Paul, 1985).

# Select Bibliography

Assagioli, Roberto. *Psychosynthesis*. New York: Penguin Books, 1971.
De Bary, William Theodore, ed. *Sources of Chinese Tradition*. New York: Columbia University Press, 1960.
Bergeron, Marie-Ina. *La Chine et Teilhard*. Paris: Editions Universitaries, Jean Pierre Delarge, 1976.
Bergson, Henri L. *Creative Evolution*. London: Macmillan & Co., Ltd., 1964.
Berry, Thomas. *Riverdale Papers*. New York: Riverdale Center for Religious Studies.
Bohm, David. *Wholeness and the Implicate Order*. London: Ark Paperbacks, 1983.
Bolen, Jean S. *The Tao of Psychology: Synchronicity*. London: Wildwood House, 1980.
*Bonaventure and the Coincidence of Opposites: The Theology of Bonaventure*. Cousins, Ewert H., ed. Chicago: Franciscan Herald Press, 1978.
Briggs, John P. and Peat, F. David. *The Looking Glass Universe*. New York: Simon and Schuster, 1984.
Brown, Lester R. *State of the World, 1984: A Worldwatch Institute Report on Progress Toward a Sustainable Society*. New York: W. W. Norton & Co., 1984.
Butterfield, Fox. *China: Alive in the Bitter Sea*. New York: Times Books, 1982.
Capra, Fritjof. *The Turning Point*. New York: Bantam Books, 1987.
Chan, Wing-Tsit. *A Source Book in Chinese Philosophy*. Princeton, NJ: Princeton University Press, 1973.
Chung-Yuan, Chang. *Tao: A New Way of Thinking. Chuang-Tzu: The Inner Chapters*. Graham, A. C., ed. London: Unwin Hyman, 1981.
*Chuang Tzu: Mystic, Moralist and Social Reformer*. Giles, Herbert A., ed. London: Bernard Quaritch, Ltd., 1926.
Coates, Gary J. *Resettling America: Energy, Ecology and Community*. Avon, MA: Brick House Publishing Co., 1981.
Colegrave, Sukie. *The Spirit of the Valley*. London: Virago Ltd., 1979.
Darwin, Charles. *On the Origin of Species*. London: Ward Lock & Co., Ltd., 1910.

Davies, Paul. *God and the New Physics*. London: J. M. Dent & Sons, Ltd., 1983.

Diebold, John. *Making the Future Work*. New York: Simon and Schuster, 1984.

Fang, Thome H. *The Chinese View of Life*. Taipei: Linking Publishing Co., Ltd., 1980.

Ferguson, Marilyn. *The Aquarian Conspiracy: Personal and Social Transformation in the 1980s*. Los Angeles: J. P. Tarcher, Inc., 1981.

Forrester, Jay. "Information Sources for Modeling the National Economy." *Journal of the American Statistical Association*, vol. 75, no. 371, 1980.

*Gaudeum et Spes*. Second Vatican Oecumenic Council, session IX, December 1965.

Geneen, Harold and Moscow, Alvin. *Managing*. New York: Doubleday & Co., Inc., 1984.

Griffiths, Bede. *The Marriage of East and West*. London: William Collins Sons & Co., Ltd., 1982.

Harman, Willis W. *An Incomplete Guide to the Future*. New York: W. W. Norton & Co., Inc., 1979.

Hawken, Paul. *The Next Economy*. New York: Holt, Rinehart and Winston, Inc., 1983.

Heidegger, Martin. *On Time and Being*. New York: Harper & Row Publishers, Inc. 1972.

Henderson, Hazel. *The Politics of the Solar Age: Alternatives to Economics*. New York: Doubleday, 1981.

Houston, Jean. *The Possible Human: A Course in Extending Your Physical, Mental and Creative Abilities*. Los Angeles: J. P. Tarcher, Inc., 1982.

Hubbard, Barbara M. *Evolutionary Journey: A Personal Guide to a Positive Future*. San Francisco: Evolutionary Press, 1982.

*Humani Generis*. (Lettre encyclique 12 Aout 1950). Discours du Pape et Chronique Romaine, supplement au no 167 Janvier 1966.

*The I Ching*. Wilhelm, Richard, ed. New York: Bollingen Foundation, Inc. and Princeton, NJ: Princeton University Press, 1968.

Jantsch, Erich. *The Self-Organizing Universe: Scientific and Human Implications of the Emerging Paradigm of Evolution*. Oxford: Pergamon Press, 1980.

Jaspers, Karl. *The Origin and Goal of History*. Michael Bullock, trans. New Haven, CT: Yale University Press, 1953.

Jung, Carl G. *An Acausal Connecting Principle*. London: Routledge & Kegan Paul, 1955.

——. *The Undiscovered Self*. London: Routledge & Kegan Paul, 1958.

King, Ursula. *Towards a New Mysticism: Teilhard de Chardin and Eastern Religions*. London: William Collins Sons & Co., Ltd., 1980.

Kuhn, Thomas. *The Structure of Scientific Revolutions*. Chicago: University of Chicago Press, 1970.

Larre, Claude. *Le Traite VII du Huai Nan Tzu*. Paris: Institut Ricci, 1982.

Lecomte de Noüy, Pierre. *Human Destiny*. Longmans, Green and Co., 1947.

Lyell, Charles. *Principles of Geology*. London: John J. Murray, 1834.

Maslow, Abraham. *Toward a Psychology of Being*. New York: Van Nos Reinhold, 1968.

McHale, Magda Cordell. *Ominous Trends and Valid Hopes: A Comparison of Five World Reports*. Minneapolis, MN: University of Minnesota, 1981.

Meadows, Dennis L. *The Limits to Growth*. New York: Universe Books, 1972.

*Les Memoires Historiques de Se-ma-Ts'ien, 1895–1905*. Paris: Leroux.

Meyer, Francois. *Teilhard et les grandes derives du monde*. Paris: Editions Universitaires, 1963.

*Mo Tzu: Basic Writings*. trans. Burton Watson. New York: Columbia University Press, 1963.

Naisbitt, John. *Megatrends*. New York: Warner Books Inc., 1988.

Needham, Joseph. *The Grand Titration: Science and Society in East and West*. London: Allen & Unwin, 1969.

——. *Science and Civilisation in China*. Cambridge: Cambridge University Press, 1972.

Peters, Thomas J. and Waterman, Robert H., Jr. *In Search of Excellence: Letters from America's Best-Run Companies*. New York: Harper & Row Publishers, Inc., 1982.

Prigogine, Ilya and Stengers, Isabelle. *Order Out of Chaos: Man's New Dialogue with Nature*. New York: Bantam Books, 1984.

Raguin, Yves. *Leçons sur le Taoisme*. Taipei: Publications de l'Association Française Pour Le Development Culturel et Scientifique en Asie, 1981.

Rawson, Philip and Legeza, Laszlo. *Tao: The Chinese Philosophy of Time and Change*. London: Thames and Hudson, 1973.

*The Resourceful Earth: A Response to Global 2000*. Simon, Julian L. and Kahn, Herman, eds. Oxford: Basil Blackwell Publishers, Ltd., 1984.

Riviere, Claude. *En Chine avec Teilhard*. Paris: Editions du Seuil, 1938–1944.

Ronan, Colin A. *The Shorter Science and Civilisation in China*. Cambridge: Cambridge University Press, 1978.

Roy, Rustin. *Experimenting with Truth*. Oxford: Pergamon Press, 1981.

Russell, Peter. *The Global Brain: Speculations on the Evolutionary Leap to Planet Consciousness*. Los Angeles: J. P. Tarcher, Inc., 1983.

——. *The Awakening Earth*. London: Routledge & Kegan Paul, 1985.

Sheldrake, Rupert. *A New Science of Life: The Hypothesis of Formative Causation*. Los Angeles: J. P. Tarcher, Inc., 1981.

Sin, R. G. H. *Ch'i: A Neo-Taoist Approach to Life*. Cambridge, MA: The MIT Press, 1974.

Spretnak, Charlene and Capra, Fritjof. *Green Politics: The Global Promise*. New York: E. P. Dutton, 1984.

Stikker, A. "Evolution and Ecology," *Futures*, Volume 22 (Number 2) (March 1990): 167–180.

Stikker, A. *Teilhard and the Industrial World*. Holland: Bres-Planete. No. 10, s'Gravenhage, 1968.

Swimme, Brian. *The Universe is a Green Dragon: A Cosmic Creation Story*. Sante Fe, NM: Bear & Co., 1985.

Teilhard de Chardin, Pierre. *The Divine Milieu*. London: William Collins Sons & Co., Ltd., and New York: Harper & Brothers, 1960.

——. *Toward the Future*. London: William Collins Sons & Co., Ltd., and New York: Harcourt Brace Jovanovich, 1975.

——. *The Phenomenon of Man*. London: William Collins Sons & Co., Ltd., and New York: Harper & Brothers, 1959.

——. *The Heart of the Matter*. London: William Collins Sons & Co., Ltd., and New York: Harcourt Brace Jovanovich, 1978.

——. *The Future of Man*. London: William Collins Sons & Co., Ltd., and New York: Harper & Row Publishers, Inc., 1964.

——. *Human Energy*. London: William Collins Sons & Co., Ltd., 1969.

——. *Mon Univers*. Paris: Editions du Seuil, 1965.

Todd, Nancy J. and Todd, John. *Bioshelters, Ocean Arks, Fish Farms: Ecology as the Basis of Design*. San Francisco: Sierra Club Books, 1984.

Toffler, Alvin. *The Adaptive Corporation*. New York: McGraw-Hill Book Co. Inc., 1985.

Wang, Dominique. *A Pekin avec Teilhard de Chardin*. Paris: Editions Robert Laffont, 1981.

Wilhelm, Richard and Jung, C. G. *The Secret of the Golden Flower: A Chinese Book of Life*. New York: Harcourt Brace Jovanovich, 1962.